MW00355155

PRAISE FOR DAVID R. EVANS AND
YIELD TO THE POWER OF COMMON SENSE

"I have known David Evans for more than forty years and we worked closely together for most of those years. Dave is one of the finest sales and marketing executives in the country. His knowledge and expertise are unparalleled. I would recommend him as an advisor or speaker to anyone in the hotel industry."

— Harry Mullikin, Former CEO of Westin Hotels and Resorts

"I have personally known Dave for more than twenty years both professionally and personally. It was my respect for him as a professional that caused our relationship to transcend from business to personal. I found Dave to be a worthy adversary. While his skills and abilities as a competitor were formidable, his gracious manner and attentive style are his most impressive attributes and rarely found. In my thirty-two years in the hotel industry, I have never seen any one better at building relationships, nor did I see a salesperson with more skill putting it to practice. He is a master."

— Darryl Hartley-Leonard, Chairman & CEO of PGI and
Former President of Hyatt Hotels & Resorts

"Ever the consummate professional, David Evans brings to the table forty years of experience in effective selling methods and excellence in customer service. His standards are high, his knowledge higher, and his ethics the highest."

— Bill Boyd, Chairman of Sunbelt Travel and
Past President of Meeting Planners International

"David Evans has been one of the industry's master communicators and outstanding leaders. His talents in market development are especially required in today's business environment. He quickly evaluates a situation and provides knowledgeable, cost-effective solutions."

— **Richard P. Fries, President and Publisher of** *Travel Agent Magazine*

"Often referred to 'Mr. Hospitality,' David Evans is one of a kind. His career as a hotelier has been marked by innovation and energy. He exemplifies relationship selling and has a reputation for giving back to society and those less fortunate. In fact, he is the model for the entire industry. Creativity, leadership, character, and style are hallmarks of his reputation."

— **David Noonan, Deputy Executive Vice President, American Academy of Ophthalmology**

"Dave Evans is a born leader and a teacher. His knowledge of the hospitality industry is unsurpassed. He has the personality to create win-win situations and to assist any group in achieving its objectives. Whether I am a leader or a follower, I want Dave on my team."

— **William Nelligan, Executive Director, Certification Board of Nuclear Cardiology, and Former Executive Vice President of the American Academy of Cardiology**

"David Evans is a highly regarded industry expert with nearly forty years of distinguished service in our industry. His energetic leadership, considerable knowledge, and active involvement on a variety of national and international boards and committees have been the hallmarks of his consistent contributions to the US travel and tourism industry."

— **William S. Norman, President & CEO, Travel Industry Association of America (TIA)**

"*Yield to the Power of Common Sense* reveals how with a little common sense we can all take control of our destinies. The wisdom David Evans learned from his decades of experience in the hotel industry can be applied to many walks of life."

— Patrick Snow, Publishing Coach and International Best-Selling Author of *Creating Your Own Destiny* and *Boy Entrepreneur*

"David Evans has had an amazing career, working with celebrities and major corporations to create major events. If this were a biography, it alone would be worth reading, but because David highlights what he learned from those experiences, *Yield to the Power of Common Sense* becomes a powerful roadmap for success."

— Tyler R. Tichelaar, PhD and Award-Winning Author of *Narrow Lives* and *The Best Place*

A COMMON SENSE ROAD MAP TO YOUR SUCCESS

YIELD TO THE POWER OF
COMMON
SENSE

$CS=PR^2$
Common Sense =
Performance & Results^2

David R. Evans CHME
SENIOR VP STARWOOD HOTELS AND RESORTS, RETIRED

Address all inquiries to:
David Evans
huskees@comcast.net
davidrevanschme.com

ISBN: 978-1-890427-39-9
Library of Congress Control Number: 2020910419

Every attempt has been made to source properly all quotes.

Published by:
Aviva Publishing
Lake Placid, NY
(518) 523-1320
www.AvivaPubs.com

AVIVA
PUBLISHING
New York

Printed in the United States of America.
First Edition
10 9 8 7 6 5 4 3 2 1

This Book is Dedicated to

My Mom and Dad for teaching me to never quit!

Bobbie, Mrs. Evans for forty-three years, and my family.

Harry Mullikin, CEO of Westin, for giving me the chance of a lifetime when he asked me to be part of the preopening team at the Century Plaza.

The incredible associates, competitors, and all in those in the meetings, conventions, corporations, associations, and travel world that I had the pleasure to work with and learn from in my career.

Patrick Snow, author of *Creating Your Own Destiny*
www.CreatingYourOwnDestiny.com

Tyler Tichelaar, editor at Superior Book Productions
www.SuperiorBookProductions.com

My dear friend Sue Allison Campbell, who prodded me to finish the book and helped design the wonderful cover.

The Good Lord, who blessed me with average intelligence so I had to learn from others!

CONTENTS

PREFACE

I am forever grateful to branding guru Duane Knapp of Brand Strategies© for sharing his branding insights with me during my active hotel career. He has written wonderful books on this subject, and his good works have long been an inspiration for me to write a book—now no longer a vision, but a reality!

We've all heard of a brand and a value proposition when we look at products and services. This book is about our *individual brand*, our individual value proposition, and how we can achieve success by using our common sense. Throughout this book I will use the equation $CS = PR^2$ (Common Sense Equals Performance and Results Squared).

Everyone on the planet is an *individual brand* because we all may have different:

- Roots
- Genders
- Languages
- Beliefs
- Upbringings
- Family values
- Skills
- Ambitions
- IQs
- Physical wellbeing
- Athletic skills

And with the advent of cellphones and social media, we may have a second brand identity that may conflict with our personal brand.

Individuals may lose their brand identities. Your good individual brand could be your demise. $CS = PR^2$ says be careful what you wish, for there may be a conflict with your individual brand and social media perception; you should check this out occasionally.

The down side of human nature is greed and a lust for power.

Reading Thomas Paine's *Common Sense* essay from 1775 was another stimulus for my writing this book. I will refer to this outstanding work throughout this book. This wonderful benchmark document was the basis for the Declaration of Independence and the US Constitution. It addresses the human lust for power over individuals and greed. Paine writes that a democratic nation, where individuals can create their individual brand identity without fear of reprisal with a representative government "of the People by the People" will succeed beyond our wildest dreams.

The United States has been a role model of success by encouraging it citizens to become individual brands.

TEN SIGNS YOU ARE DOING WELL IN LIFE
(Even if you don't feel like it)
— Author Unknown

1. You have a roof over your head.
2. You ate today.
3. You have a good heart.
4. You wish good for others.
5. You have clean water.
6. Someone cares for you.
7. You forgive others.
8. You have clean clothes.
9. You stay in faith.
10. You're breathing.

This book is intended to help prepare you for whatever success you desire in life by giving you a roadmap for success. That roadmap is $CS = PR^2$. With it, I trust you will be able to create an individual brand and value proposition.

I wish you luck in your journey!

Dave R. Evans

David R. Evans, CHME (Certified Hotel Marketing Executive)

"The best classroom in the world is at the feet of an elderly person."

— Andy Rooney

INTRODUCTION

THE POWER OF COMMON SENSE CS = PR²

"Today is a seven. You're a sponge for knowledge, so pass on whatever you have learned—your common sense could carry you a long way."
— My horoscope for Sunday, April 12, 2012

"Common sense is not so common."
— Voltaire

I started this book six years ago, but I took a hiatus when my spouse of fifty-two years, Bobbie, passed away on February 8, 2014. And then I had some medical challenges, but I wanted to finish this unfinished business, so I give my thanks to my dear friend Sue Allison Campbell who pressed me to finish it this past May of 2020.

Notably, in the six years since I began it, common sense has given way even more to political correctness (PC).

Several years ago, the following was printed in the *London Times*.

Obituary: The Sad Passing of Common Sense

Today, we mourn the passing of a beloved old friend, Common Sense, who has been with us for many years.

No one knows for sure how old he was, since his birth records were long ago lost in bureaucratic red tape. He will be remembered as having cultivated such valuable lessons as knowing when to come in out of the rain, why the early bird gets the worm, life isn't always fair, and maybe it was my fault.

Common Sense lived by simple, sound financial policies (don't spend more than you can earn) and reliable strategies (adults, not children, are in charge).

His health began to deteriorate rapidly when well-intentioned but overbearing regulations were set in place. Reports of an 8 year-old boy charged with sexual harassment for kissing a classmate; teens suspended from school for using mouthwash after lunch; and a teacher fired for reprimanding an unruly student, only worsened his condition.

Common Sense lost ground when parents attacked teachers for doing the job that they themselves had failed to do in disciplining their unruly children.

It declined even further when schools were required to get parental consent to administer sun lotion or an aspirin to a student, but could not inform parents when a student became pregnant and wanted to have an abortion.

Common Sense lost the will to live as the Ten Commandments became contraband, the churches became businesses; and criminals received better treatment than their victims.

Common Sense took a beating when you couldn't defend yourself from a burglar in your own home and the burglar could sue you for assault.

Common Sense finally gave up the will to live, after a woman failed to realize that a steaming cup of coffee was hot. She spilled a little in her lap and was promptly awarded a huge settlement.

Common Sense was preceded in death, by his parents, Truth and Trust, by his wife, Discretion, by his daughter, Responsibility, and by his son, Reason.

He is survived by three stepbrothers: I Know My Rights, Someone Else Is to Blame, and I'm a Victim.

Not many attended his funeral because so few realized he was gone. If you still remember him, pass this on. If not, join the majority and do nothing.

To express conservative values—to respect our flag, anthem, hard work, limited government, and freedom of speech—is viewed as radical today and such expressions are often stifled. Every disagreement is vilified. We are losing the ability to disagree without being disagreeable.

Great decisions and accomplishments are made when they are hatched in an atmosphere from which freely flows open, honest, and direct feedback.

Those wishing to tear up our common sense declaration of independence are doing so for one reason: power!

Power to control your lives, power to control dissent, and power for power's sake.

Power corrupts. Absolute power corrupts absolutely!

How do we fight power? Ronald Reagan said it well: "No arsenal or weapon in the arsenals of the world is as formidable as the will and courage of free men and women."

$CS = PR^2$ says:

- We should be blessed and thankful that our forefathers created the free democracy we have today!
- We should feel blessed with the vision of public education for all!
- We should feel blessed with vision to create our wonderful land-grant universities with our public universities!
- We should feel blessed that we have the ability to be whatever we want to be—to change what is bad and improve what is good!
- We should feel blessed that we don't live in an autocratic society with a dictator; we are free to think and speak as we please! We can vote for our elected officials, and if we don't vote, we must be prepared to suffer the consequences.

With this book, I hope to point out that the power of common sense ($CS = PR^2$) will always win the day.

This book comes from my forty-five years in the world of hospitality. I can't think of any other industry that is a better example of where common sense, used day to day, is the correct way of operating and doing business. The world of hospitality is still using common sense during day-to-day operations, while many other industries now use data and technology, taking the human touch and interaction out of the equation.

Einstein created $E = MC^2$. I, David R. Evans, created $CS = PR^2$ (Common Sense = Performance and Results Squared). I wish to clarify, however, that in no way am I comparing myself to the genius of Albert Einstein. I was blessed with average intelligence and an insatiable curiosity to learn from history and those much smarter than me.

My intentions with this book are to show that a simple formula, $CS = PR^2$, can be a life-changer.

I have included case studies and examples from former associates, competitors, and industry leaders. Throughout, I have also scattered numerous common sense quotations that have made an impression on me. I trust they will do the same for you.

There is nothing new in this book, only a reaffirmation that as human beings—blessed with the gift of reasoning, unlike animals, who are blessed with instincts—we have an advantage. However, when we let our egos, ambitions, and emotions (including political correctness) get in the way of common sense, thereby clouding good judgment, we make uncalled for mistakes.

According to Robert A. Rosen in *Leading People*, "Common sense, albeit in life, and one's career, leadership, or management may be simple to understand but hard to master. It requires constant introspection, peeling back the layers of one's self—learning about one's weaknesses and strengths." In short, common sense requires contemplation and challenge, hard thinking and hard knocks.

This book shares what I have been pondering for the past twenty years since I retired. It is based on lessons I learned from successes and hard knocks over my forty-seven years in the hospitality industry and the lessons I gained from my best teachers, bosses, customers, competitors, family members, and friends.

The road to achieving common sense is littered with examples of egotistic, emotional, and ambitious leaders who have led their corporations and countries down the road to doom and failure.

During the eighteen years since my retirement, I have noticed that in all walks of life, business and family common sense have gone the way of political correctness. "Spare the rod and spoil the child," "good manners," and "reasonable dissent" have all been brushed aside. A couple of years ago, an old friend suggested I read Thomas Paine's February 14, 1775 essay on common sense: "Why America Must Become Independent."

I was so moved by what Thomas Paine was able to articulate in about fifty pages in this extraordinary document, the genesis for the Declaration of Independence, that I decided to write this book. It was then I created the concept of CS = PR².

Today, the IRS tax code is one hundred times longer than Thomas Paine's fifty-page document. We need to be wary of too much government, with dictators, kings, and queens creating thousands of rules and regulations, and having too much central control. A perfect example of too much government is how it takes one one-hundred-foot tree just to finance a house.

So I started to put some common sense ideas together.

During my retirement, I have seen hate-organized protests, journalism become an opinion, a failure to report news, millennials disallowed free speech (at the University of California), and rejection of the ultimate symbol of world freedom: "The Stars and Stripes."

I have seen NFL players who receive multimillion-dollar paychecks not respecting the national anthem because of political correctness. Our college students are being taught by left-leaning, socialist professors, and our youth from kindergarten to twelfth grade are not studying history. Common sense tells me they have never read Thomas Paine or any history books.

So this is my book on common sense. The CS = PR² lessons are those I learned as a youngster growing up in West Vancouver, Canada during World War II. I worked hard at every stage in my life, including in college and during the forty-seven years I spent in the hospitality business.

Throughout my career, I have been inspired by my Westin Hotels and Resorts and Starwood Hotels and Resorts associates, my industry, corporations, association leaders, competitors, and historical figures. They prompted me to put my thoughts to paper to share the common-sense thread that comes through all success stories.

So this is an attempt to add a footnote to my career.

The many who contributed to this book are listed in the acknowledgments.

I would be very remiss, however, if I didn't recognize my father, who was a very successful businessman, and also an accomplished stage actor.

When I was eleven, I saw him onstage in Vancouver, BC, playing Willy Loman, the lead role in Arthur Miller's classic play, *Death of Salesman*. At that time, I was too young to understand the play's real meaning. Only later, when I read a synopsis of the play in *Newsweek*, as it was being resurrected on Broadway in 2012 by Mike Nichols, did I realize that *in fact, I was a Willy Loman*.

In the March 2012 *Omnivore*, Sam Tanenhaus wrote an article titled, "A Nation of Willy Lomans." In it, he states:

> Miller's play isn't ideological at all. There is not a whiff in it of anti-capitalist "critique." Its subject, at once deeper and less abstract, is the American myth of self-invention or reinvention, the dreams and delusions it fosters in us, which lead us away from our true selves. "Willy has chosen to follow the craft that is not a craft, and he has a craft," Nichols says. "The sad thing about it is, as his sons know, there are things he's very good at—carpentry, building, putting in a ceiling in his house. But he doesn't have any respect for that. What he thinks is important is to be able to sell, to convince, to charm, and it's one of the things that's wrong with us now. If you go into any office and ask people, 'What exactly is it that you do?' they either say, 'I record the numbers, and then I put them in another book,' or they say, 'I have ideas. I have ideas for commercials, promotion.' We basically are promoting our product."

One of Miller's most inspired touches is, that he never tells us, nor do we think to ask, what's inside the heavy sample cases Willy lugs into the house and then on the road. We don't ask because the answer is obvious. The "product" he's peddling is himself. This is the theology, still with us today, of the post-Depression middle class, and its scripture was written not by Adam Smith in *The Wealth of Nations* but by Dale Carnegie (*How to Win Friends and Influence People*) and Bruce Barton (*The Man Nobody Knows*) in which Jesus is described as "the founder of modern business." In his own mind, Willy Loman is not an "entrepreneur." He is a buccaneer "way out there in the blue, riding on a smile and a shoeshine." Nichols sees Willy's pathetic need to be "well liked...."

Perhaps, this description of how Willy operates best describes my days of hospitality sales learning. I went often by the seat of my pants and, sometimes, learned from my mistakes and from others as I went along, but like Wilily Loman, "riding on a smile and a shoeshine," I wanted to be liked by my customers and perhaps use some common sense along the way.

I trust you will find this primer on common sense beneficial, and hopefully, it will help you close deals and make you a better leader, manager, politician, parent, and, above all, a better individual.

Here's a CS = PR^2 metaphor that has application to this book.

King Henry V of England, realizing he was vastly outnumbered 25,000 to 15,000 on October 25, 1415, coming off a victory on the coast of France at Harfleur a month earlier with a better strategy and tactics, changed warfare forever. France's 15,000 armored knights were no match for Henry's Welsh bowmen. Common sense says when you are faced with what appears to be overwhelming odds, expect the unexpected.

The day was won at Agincourt by the undermanned English Army in three hours because the arrogant French did not expect the 5,000 armor-piercing arrows that decimated them.

This book on common sense is my "Agincourt."

I will have won my victory if the CS = PR^2 lessons win your hearts and minds.

CS = PR²
INTRODUCTION TAKEAWAYS

- We should be blessed and thankful that our forefathers created the free democracy we have today!
- We should be blessed with the vision of public education for all!
- We should be blessed with vision to create our wonderful "land grant universities" with our public universities!
- We should be blessed, with the ability to be whatever we want to be—to change what is bad and improve what is good!
- We should be blessed that we don't live in an autocratic society with a dictator; we are free to think and speak as we please! We can vote for our elected officials, and if we don't vote, we can be prepared to suffer the consequences.
- History is a mirror.
- A little common sense goes a long way.

What three or more lessons did you from this introduction?

1. _____

2. _____

3. _____

PART 1

COMMON SENSE LESSONS LEARNED IN SALES, MANAGEMENT, AND LEADERSHIOP

1

WHAT I LEARNED IN MY CAREER

"I was blessed to be in the right place at the right time."

— David R. Evans

"The difference between a successful person and others is not a lack of strength but rather a lack of will."

— Vince Lombardi

I would be less than honest if I did not acknowledge that my success has largely been due to good timing and being in the right place at the right time. In my career, I was blessed to meet so many successful people, and learn that selling is the art of building relationships and getting and closing the deal from very capable competitors.

And I had the good fortune of having thirty-nine extraordinary years with Western International Hotels. Unfortunately, I had unplanned retirement due heart failure. When I told my Starwood boss, Fred Kleisner, President of Starwood Hotels and Resorts, during the opening of the first new "W" in New York in 1999, he was silent for two minutes. Then he said, "I'm so sorry to learn this.

It does change things somewhat." Fred was very kind and deeply concerned about my medical situation going forward.

I was the last man standing at Westin, except for my very capable assistant, Andre Gillis. A representative from the Sheraton Seattle came in at 11:00 a.m. on March 31, 2000, to shut down our computer, closing the seventy-five-year history of Western International Hotels (Westin) headquarters in Seattle. Founded in 1929, it was the second oldest management company in the business. Conrad Hilton had started Hilton one year earlier in 1928.

This was my last day on the job. I went home at noon to wait for a new heart.

Juergen Bartells, Starwood CEO, and Fred Kleisner, Starwood President, were very gracious when setting my plans for this early retirement, Fred said, "It will take more than one person to replace you." Well, it did. Due to my pending transplant as Starwood Senior Vice President, I assisted in locating my three replacements: Bob Moore, Executive Vice President Sales and Marketing; Christy Hicks, Senior Vice President Sales; and David Scypinski, Vice President of Sales.

Bob and David were former Hilton Associates. Christy came from Hyatt.

On August 25, 2000, after two years of heart failure and waiting, I had a very successful heart transplant at the University of Washington Medical Center.

The morning of the surgery, the hospital called and told me it had a new heart for me. I only knew I'd have a heart transplant the day it happened, and I had to go to the hospital immediately. As my oldest son Greg drove me there, he asked, "How do you feel, Dad?" I responded with the following statements:

- "I have a clear conscience, having never knowingly done anyone harm in my career.

- I did the best job possible without trying to work within corporate politics or attempting to impress my bosses: 'Actions speak louder than words.'
- I have taken very good care of my family.
- I am having the surgery in the number one place for successful transplants in the nation.
- I feel relieved, Greg. The long wait is over. *I am not worried a bit!'*

My hotel sales road was like the Yellow Brick Road—a magic carpet that allowed me at a very young age to develop relationships and interact on a frequent basis with CEOs of such major companies as Anheuser Busch, Boeing, the NFL (including commissioner Pete Rozelle and his wife Carrie), the American Broadcasting Company, the Columbia Broadcasting System, and the National Broadcasting Company, Twentieth-Century Fox, Warner Brothers, American International Pictures, Pabst Blue Ribbon, Olympia Brewing Company, Equitable Life Insurance, and Chrysler.

Among the wonderful association executives, who lead our nation's industry and medical associations, I had the good fortune to establish extraordinary personal relationships with Jim Low, Executive Vice President, and Bill Taylor, who followed Jim Lowe as Executive Vice President at the American Society of Association Executives. I also knew Roy Evans, who was an Executive of the American Society of Association Executives (ASAE) and Executive Vice President, of the Professional Convention Management Association (PCMA). And I knew Ed Griffin, President and CEO of Meeting Planner International (MPI). They all became close friends and mentors.

Among politicians, I got to meet and know Los Angeles Mayor Sam Yorty, California Governor/President Ronald Reagan, and President George H. Bush.

I had the pleasure to work with and learn from many well-known celebrities in an upfront and personal way. I met them outside of their acting work environment as real people. They include

Debbie Reynolds, a dedicated chair of the "City of Hope" charity. Western films star Dale Robertson, who was the honorary Mayor of Santa Monica, and Gregory Peck, President of the "Screen Actors Guild" (SAG). I was well prepared by my part-time actor father not to have stars in my eyes since we had many celebrities in our home in West Vancouver, British Columbia, when I was growing up.

I met many other celebrities who were involved with our local community charities, including Lorne Greene, Artie Johnson, John Wayne, Bob Hope, Bing Crosby, Monty Hall, Adam West (Batman), and Julie Andrews.

They were all frequent guests of the hotel whom I assisted over time with special events and VIP reservations.

$CS = PR^2$ Lesson:
Turning your clients into friends is the formula for success.

During this magic carpet ride, I had the good fortune to:
- Be selected as the hotel's industry representative as a member on the Board of the American Society of Association Executives (ASAE), following my good friends and competitors Joe Kordsmeier Vice President-Sales (Hyatt) and John Metcalfe, Vice President-Sales (Fairmont)
- Serve on the board of the Professional Convention Management Association (PCMA) and be the first supplier to serve on PCMA's executive committee, selected by Brad Claxton CEO of American Academy of Dermatology as PCMA Chairman.
- Be a founding member of the Meeting Planners International Board of Directors and the PCMA Foundation.

Without doubt, the common sense lessons I learned from my parents, my grandparents, and their friends, beginning at the age of thirteen, led to my success. Beginning at that age I was interacting with people of all levels of success in BC Collateral (our family business and the second largest pawn shop in Canada). I met everyone from loggers and fishermen to the wealthy elite. My mother's gracious manner and superb hostess skills and my dad's extraordinary ability to build relationships and interact without fear at any level had an enormous impact on me.

My father, Alfred A. Evans, besides being an accomplished actor and a violinist, was an outstanding business man with superb selling skills. We always said, "He could sell a fridge to an Eskimo in January."

I learned a valuable sales lesson from my father. By reading and understanding history, we can learn from the past. My father was an avid historian, and it rubbed off on me, creating my insatiable curiosity. Curiosity is one of most important traits of a successful salesperson because salespeople must ask questions and get to know the person they are trying to get to buy their product.

History also aided me in sales because it taught me not to let rejection get you down. History is filled with examples of failures that were followed by success.

CS = PR² Lesson: The art of selling is listening. Get to know your client. Curiosity may have killed the cat, but never a salesperson.

When I joined the sales department at the Olympic Hotel in Seattle on September 17, 1961, the hotel sales profession was still in its infancy. Starting in New York after World War II, when I entered the industry, hotel sales was strong in New York City, Chicago, and Miami. It was a new phenomenon for hotels in the Midwest and on the West Coast.

The hotel market had changed after World War II. Competition was developing everywhere in the country, so hotels had to create sales teams to go out and get business. As a result, Western International Hotels (WIH) was forced to create sales teams in its hotels. WIH pioneered the hotel business in many ways, leading the way to the first reservation system and later central reservation system and certified reservations, plus credit card usage, twenty-four-hour room service, and specialty restaurants. However, when I joined direct sales, sales teams in hotels was a new activity in WIH hotels, having just begun in the mid-1950s. Prior to that, most hotel marketing, advertising, and public relations was geared toward catering.

At the time I was hired, I was working on a directors training program, on a job made in heaven for recent alumni of the University of Washington's School of Communications at Seattle's first TV station, KING-TV.

Late in the summer of 1961, someone told me about a public relations job at the Western International's Olympic Hotel in Seattle.

I'd already had a taste of the hotel business while in high school, in West Vancouver, BC, at a wonderful resort, sixty miles east of Vancouver—the Harrison Hot Springs Hotel. What intrigued me about this new opportunity at the Olympic was the important people I might meet. A light went on that while working at the Olympic, I might meet someone visiting from the motion picture or TV industry, who might "pull me through looking glass" and offer me a job in motion pictures or TV production in Los Angeles.

So, after three wonderful months at KING-TV, I made the big leap and came to the Olympic, only to find that, in fact, it was a hospitality sales job. That was even better than a public relations position because it provided a great opportunity to meet people. This started my hotel career, which would span forty-seven years. The Olympic Hotel sales team became the benchmark sales team for all other sales teams in Western International Hotels.

Departing King TV was not easy. When I made my decision known, Lee Shulman, Executive Producer, returned promptly from a major production at the Puyallup Fair to spend three-plus hours discussing with me the pros and cons of my decision.

While disappointed when I still decided to leave, Lee wished me well and we parted on good terms. I had learned a valuable lesson from my father: "Don't burn bridges." Later, when I was Director of Sales at the Century Plaza, Lee Shulman, who been promoted to VP of NBC on the West Coast, was instrumental in helping me move the West Coast Emmys from the Beverly Hilton to the Century Plaza.

CS = PR² Lesson: Don't burn bridges.
Today's challenge may be tomorrow's success.

We can always expect to go the down the Yellow Brick Road in the direction we plan like Dorothy and her friends do in *The Wizard of Oz*. However, sometimes things in life take us in a different direction. Dorothy wanted to go to the Emerald City, but she never expected to go to the Wicked Witch of the West's castle. But only by fighting the witch, which was a big risk, was she finally able to go home. Without risk, there is no gain.

Here's a CS = PR² story from my longtime friend David Brudney, owner of David Brudney & Associates, and a former Century Plaza sales associate. He shares a tale of how without some risk, there is no gain.

My example of a common sense practice goes back to my very first consulting assignment some thirty-four years ago. I was still employed by Hyatt Hotels, but I was teaching a class in hotel and restaurant management and marketing at UCLA Extension. One of my students approached me after class and wanted to hire me as a consultant to help him with his takeout pizza and roasted chicken store he and his sons owned and operated in South Pasadena.

I agreed, although I felt more than a little unqualified for the task. I showed up one afternoon at Big Man Pizza, across the street from a supermarket, and sandwiched between a laundromat and a corner tavern.

I had no prior F&B (food and beverage) marketing experience outside a hotel, but I was impressed that my student—the owner, Chuck Fata—had the confidence to hire me.

I looked around the 1,000-square foot store and thought to myself, *Where to begin? What should I look at? What should I ask?* Chuck asked, "David, where do you want to start?" Common sense told me to begin with Big Man's existing clientele.

"Let's take a look at your phone records first," I said. "Why would you want to do that?" asked Chuck, with a bewildered look on his face. I told him that since 90 percent of his business came from customer call-ins, we needed to learn from phone prefixes where his customers lived and worked. When he was still puzzled, I told him he might want to begin delivering printed flyers in those targeted neighborhoods and offices to develop new incremental business.

Next, I went over upselling on the phone—something he and his sons knew nothing about. Again, it just was a case of common sense.

It was obvious to me to present this practice. They instantly realized their past missed opportunities for doubling a pizza order with a half-chicken, or tripling orders with three different types of pizza.

A follow-up session led me to recommend he use the 250-square feet of wasted space at the entrance for a product display case, and by adding small benches, counters, and stools, he could provide a place for customers to dine right there. Later, I encouraged him to seek a beer and wine license.

I had no training for what I did. It was basically "flying by the seat of my pants." Common sense at its best! Yes, I'm sure my hotel sales and marketing experience and training helped. Closing note: Less than six months later, the store doubled its revenue.

And my new professional consulting career was launched with Big Man Pizza. Chuck Fata was not only my very first client, but he became a lifetime client.

CS = PR² Lesson: No risk, no gain!

I spent four wonderful years at the Olympic Hotel learning the ropes in operations and sales from Tom Gildersleeve, Managing Director; Pat Foley, Front Office Manager (later to be CEO of Hyatt Hotels); Catering Manager, Norm Lavin; and the hotel sales team: Bill Newman (Later Westin SVP); Gordon Stenness (moved on to brand X Hyatt); and Director of Sales, Don Allison (later manager of WIH properties and then CEO of Caesars' Palace in Las Vegas).

The year 1964 was a fateful one for me. That was when Harry Mullikin, Westin Vice President, who had been promoted to VP Managing Director of the planned new spectacular Century Plaza Hotel (CPH) to be located in "Century City," tapped me to be part of the pre-opening sales team. The new Century City was to be located on the former backlot of Twentieth Century Fox, a new development by ALCOA and Twentieth Century Fox. The CPH was scheduled to open in April 1966.

So, in the winter of 1964, my pregnant spouse Bobbie, our first child, Gregory, and I left the apartment we loved in Madison Park, a residential area on Lake Washington in Seattle, and drove to the bright lights of Hollywood and West Los Angeles to start the most exciting part of my early career in the hotel business at the Century Plaza Hotel.

John Moore was the first Director of Sales at the Century Plaza Hotel when I arrived in 1964. He resigned in 1965 and was replaced by Bruce McKibbin, who had been promoting the CPH in Chicago.

I spent the first year and half as a member of the pre-opening sales team. Because of my TV and entertainment background, I was assigned the motion picture and TV market segment.

In early May 1966, out of the clear blue, I received a call from VP Managing Director Harry Mullikin's secretary, the ever-gracious Penny Scott. She asked me to deliver a backboard to his home in fashionable Bel Air for his chronic back pain. I was mumbling all the way to his house from the Century Plaza pre-opening offices in Century City, thinking I was being treated just like an errand boy. Little did I realize my career path and life were about to change forever.

Destiny was on my side.

On that fateful day, Harry was at his home, suffering from back pain. After some small talk and "Thanks for schlepping the back board," he told me the real reason for my visit was to discuss changes coming in the CPH's sales department. I was sitting and listening, when he said, "I am making you Director of Sales and Bruce McKibbin our first company VP of Sales and Marketing."

To say I was in shock is putting it mildly. I reflected on my nasty thoughts driving up to Harry's house, apologizing in my mind, while trying to grasp the scope of what was about to happen and how my life would change. *I ate my words, in exuberance, all the way back to the hotel.*

I spent eight exciting years as Director of Sales at the Century Plaza, the first hotel in the United States to receive the prestigious Mobile Five Star, rating within the first year of operation.

The new Century City was bordered between Santa Monica Boulevard (adjacent to Beverly Hills) on its north, and on its south side, Olympic Boulevard in West Los Angeles, It was also between the fashionable Los Angeles Country Club (north) and the Hillcrest Country Club (south), the latter a predominantly Jewish club where Jack Benny and his counterparts in the entertainment industry were members.

While my first year as Director of Sales was filled with anxiety and some team challenges, we built a great team of hotel sales professionals: David Brudney, Pat O'Daniel, Bruce Lucker, Steve Gold, David Falor, and Stan Soroka. Our stellar team of assistants consisted of Jean Kappert (my secretary), Pat Simanski, Susan Pfister, Marie Mickelbart, Maggie Hope, and Jean Robinson, but the glue that held this good ship together was the venerable Charlene Chabin, office administrator. (Rumor had it she also mowed my lawn.)

Later, we added Linda Sperber to handle the corporate travel market. She became the best corporate sales manager in the company. We fondly called Linda "Squirely." She was an organizational mess, but she could sell, and the corporate clients loved her.

Our goal was for the CPH to be the best hotel in the company. Each associate on our outstanding sales team would eventually move on too much bigger assignments with great success. I remember so well how we worked together like a band of brothers and sisters. It reminds me of a wonderful passage from Shakespeare's *Henry V*:

We few, we happy few, we band of brothers;
For he to-day that sheds his blood with me
Shall be my brother; be he ne'er so vile,
This day shall gentle his condition;
And gentlemen in England now a-bed
Shall think themselves accurs'd they were not here,
And hold their manhoods cheap whiles any speaks
That fought with us upon Saint Crispin's day.

We fought our sales battles in a very competitive marketplace and won the day.

One of the first things I did was move our sales meeting from 9 a.m. Thursday to 8 a.m., Saturday. That way, the meetings were always quick and focused on action because we were all anxious for a weekend break.

I learned a very valuable lesson during that fateful visit with Harry Mullikin at his home. He told me something that resonated with me for my whole career: "Give your team the tools and let them do their jobs." He told me my sales budget was sacrosanct between him and me. My sales office budget was fluid, and my job was to spend it wisely to reach and exceed our goals and objectives.

Harry, practicing excellent CS = PR² leadership, let us do our jobs with one goal that I used later in my career as a management benchmark.

CS = PR² Lesson: Give your team the tools and let them do their jobs.
CS = PR² Lesson: Be over plan in production by 10 percent and under plan by 10 percent with your budget.

To put it simply, he let us do our thing! This led to innovation and creativity. The CPH sales team created a lot of firsts for WIH. We were the first sales team to consistently produce group business with an average daily rate (ADR) that exceeded the individual business and Front Desk ADR by $10.00 or more.

CS = PR² Lesson: Don't micromanage and stifle your subordinates.

At the Century Plaza, all associates and executives were encouraged to think outside the box. As a result, we were the first and only non-Twentieth Fox studio organization to have an event on the back lot of Twentieth-Century Fox, located on the Western set of the iconic film *Stagecoach*. It was the closing event for our annual WIH sales meeting in the spring of 1971.

My good friend Lorne Greene provided his extras from the TV series *Gunsmoke* for our event, making this evening a once-in-a-lifetime experience. The *Gunsmoke* extras not only playacted to start the event, but they became a part of our celebration and mingled with our sales associates.

This Western International annual sales meeting final "fun night" event was the talk of the company for years to come.

We also created the first sales department planning system. I credit my Director of Sales predecessor Bruce McKibbin with conceiving the idea, but I developed the finished product on my dining room table at my home. For years, it was the benchmark system at WIH.

CS = PR² Lesson: Be prepared to take on a challenge and innovate.

I was successful in moving *TV Guide*'s annual "Press Tours" from the Beverly Hilton to the Century Plaza.

I agreed to let the organizers use the garden area around the pool for the interviews. They set up on Sunday morning. At 7 a.m. on Monday, I was checking to see if they were all set for the first interviews when Harry Mullikin tapped me on my shoulder. He was not a happy camper when he saw movie lights, cameras, and cables all over the outdoor patio and pool area.

"David what is this all about?" he asked.

I told him it was for the interviews for the new *TV Guide* business we had just taken from the Beverly Hilton, and I added, "This is what our guests expect when they come to Los Angeles—lights, camera, action!"

This statement soothed him.

The next year, and for ten years following, the interviews were moved to our penthouse suites for more privacy. After that, the interviews were moved to New York.

CS = PR² Lesson: Think outside the box when confronted with a challenging situation. It is better to ask for forgiveness than apologize for failure.

Every year, the networks conducted affiliates meetings. At the time, cable television did not exist, and the networks were only allowed to own five stations so there was heavy competition to keep their affiliated stations in the "family." These annual gatherings boiled down to: Who can outdo who during three days of wining and dining? For us, because the competition was very happy to keep other networks' affiliate stations happy, these meetings were high revenue generators.

First, I was successful in moving the affiliate meetings for the American Broadcasting Company (ABC) in May 1967 from the Ambassador Hotel in the mid-Wilshire area and from the Beverly Hilton to the Century Plaza. Later, CBS and NBC's affiliate meetings also moved.

From the day we signed our confirmation letter to the day the ABC Affiliates meeting started at the hotel in May 1967, not one single piece of paper prior to the meeting was exchanged between the ABC meeting planner, Vice President, Milton Carney, and myself.

Those were simpler days. We had no long legal contracts, only handshakes and a short one-page "sign and return" letter confirming dates of arrival and departure and number of rooms. This was the standard operating procedure (SOP). This situation changed in the early 1980s when the lawyers got involved. Oddly, we never had any litigious issues until they entered the picture.

Meeting arrangements were made by phone. Milton would call me, and then I would dictate the information to my secretary, who would type it up and pass it on to our outstanding Director of Convention Services, Bodo Lemke. Bodo was not only "world class best" at his job, but the first convention services manager in the company.

Each meeting concluded with an elegant, star-studded banquet. CPH's banquet service standard was a modified "French service," meaning individual service for each course. Mandatory attendance was required by the TV celebrities and the price was no object. Our extraordinary executive chef, Walter Roth, and his outstanding team of culinarians, along with our banquet manager, Frank Aprent and his team of service associates, did an outstanding job with our modified French service to ensure every network affiliate event was world class.

My dream of meeting someone in the TV business became a reality in 1971, following our third American Broadcasting affiliates meeting, when ABC Vice President John Gilbert offered me a job at the network. We met in his suite for about an hour where he explained to me that the job was in affiliate relations and could lead to a position in TV production. I asked him if I could discuss it with my spouse, Bobbie, and told him I'd give him my decision the next day.

Bobbie convinced me my future was with Westin and the hotel sales and marketing field. So I told John I was deeply flattered, but I was going to stay at Century Plaza. He wished me the best, and we became longtime friends. When I retired in 2000, ABC was the Century Plaza's longest and most valued customer/friend.

CS = PR² Lesson: Don't burn bridges.
Today's challenge may be tomorrow's success.

The three network executives, Milton Carney (ABC), Mike Laurence (NBC), and Bob Woods (CBS) also became lifelong friends, and each was a character in his own way.

The real key to the Century Plaza's success was its world class convention services manager, Bobo Lemke. He made sure all the pieces of the puzzle were in place. There was no one better at this job in the entire country than Bobo Lemke! Sadly, this exceptional Westin executive passed away in 2017.

I had a unique opportunity as a young sales manager at the Century Plaza when I booked the first convention into the hotel twice—*yes, twice.* I had booked the National Swimming Pool Institute for April 1, 1966, the date of the hotel's scheduled opening. However, it was not to be. Coming to work in mid-March 1966, I noticed the construction elevator was not working. When I made inquiries, I learned the elevator workers were on strike. I had to call Bob Steele, Executive Vice President of the National

Swimming Pool Institute and tell him to cancel or move his convention. Bob moved his convention and trade show to Caesar's Palace in Las Vegas. The Century Plaza's opening would then be delayed two months.

Late in April 1966, I received a call out of the blue from Lou Bell, Executive Director of the fledgling travel trailer organization, Trailer Coach Association (TCA). He wanted to book a new show and we did! TCA group checked in on Friday, June 1, 1966, the first day the Century Plaza opened its doors. We opened 100 percent fully occupied that weekend, and the first event in our sparkling new 20,000-square-foot ballroom was a trade show.

On Sunday, June 3 around 7 a.m., while I was checking to see how everything was going, Harry Mullikin told me he was not very happy to see his new spectacular ballroom opening with exhibits, but since the hotel opened at 100 percent occupancy, he would give me a pass.

TCA became an annual event at the Century Plaza for years, until it got too large and moved to Dodger Stadium.

An interesting challenge came along in 1968, the third year the TCA trade show was held at CPH.

That year, thanks to the great work of Resident Manager Dan McClaskey and the vision of Harry Mullikin, the Century Plaza became the "Western White House." Dan and Harry worked very closely with the Secret Service to create the most secure hotel in the West. Presidents Lyndon B. Johnson and Ronald Reagan would both make the Century Plaza their "home away from home" when visiting Southern California.

However, the challenge came in the form of an early morning call in April 1968, from Dan McClaskey. He told me the Secret Service had contacted him. It wanted to move Democratic presidential candidate Robert Kennedy's planned visit to the Ambassador Hotel to the Century Plaza. The Secret Service knew full well the Century Plaza was the securest hotel in Los Angeles.

This was an extraordinary and very prestigious opportunity for us; however, it would mean having to cancel the TCA trade show at the CPH and would give Lou Bell only two months to move the show to a new location.

I called Lou to see if he could move. He was understanding, so he checked out the alternatives; however, in the end, he told me it was far too late to move the TCA show.

When I told Dan, "I talked with Lou Bell and he advised me he could not move his trade show," Dan was not happy. "David, move them!" he told me.

But I stood my ground. I told him I couldn't ask Lou to move the show, and the hotel could fire me if it had to.

Robert Kennedy's planned visit would remain at the Ambassador Hotel.

Once again that magic carpet appeared. My fateful walk down the Yellow Brick Road remained on track. I was not fired.

A couple of months later, on June 5, 1968, I heard the news on the radio that Robert F. Kennedy had been shot at the Ambassador Hotel. I paused and shook. I felt a sense of guilt. Had I moved the TCA trade show and had Kennedy stayed at the Century Plaza, given our extraordinary security, Robert Kennedy might have still been alive. This tragedy may have been averted, or worse yet, the assassination might have occurred at the Century Plaza. In the end, I was relieved I had honored my commitment to the trade show.

CS = PR² Lesson: Honor your commitments. Stand your ground if you think you are doing the right thing. Doing the right thing is more important than doing things right.

During my early days as director of sales, I took Harry Mullikin's sound direction seriously. When he told me I should "learn from the best" and suggested I join the local chapter of the Hotel Sales Management Association (HSMA), I did. I then attended the national meeting and set out to meet and learn from the best. Among them were:

- Sig Front, Vice President Sales and Marketing, Sahara Hotel, Las Vegas
- John Monahan, Executive Vice President, Diplomat Hotel, Miami
- Ed Sansovini, Senior Vice President Sales, Leamington Hotel, St Louis
- Frank Berkman, Executive Director, Hotel Sales Management Association (HSMA)
- Ben Gould, Senior Vice President, Biltmore Hotel, Los Angeles
- Steve Sherrill, Director of Sales, Beverly Hilton Hotel, Beverly Hills
- George Harbaugh, Vice President Sales, Biltmore Hotel, and later the new Los Angeles Airport Hotel

In 1968, I became President of the Southern California Hotel Sales Management Association (HSMA) Chapter, started the Westin Region HSMA, joined forces with the NorCal HSMA Chapter, and served as board member of the International HSMA Association.

Andy Rooney, Emmy award-winning journalist for 60 Minutes, once said, "The best classroom in the world is at the feet of an elderly person." For me, my best classroom was at the feet of these industry giants.

I would here like to express my great gratitude to a very special group of CPH leaders and department heads, who made our sales team look good with our customer-friends. They embodied August Busch's saying, "Making friends was our business."

- Dan McClaskey, Resident Manager
- Penny Scott, Executive Assistant to Harry Mullikin
- Gina Tucker, Executive Housekeeper
- Walter Roth, Executive Chef
- Larry Magnan, Rooms Division Manager

- Peter Blyth, Director of Food and Beverage
- William "Bill" D. Ellis, Controller

In 1971, I was very surprised when the CPH sales team, the supporting cast of sales support associates, and the Western International Hotels (WIH) leaders nominated me for the Washington State Hotel School's prestigious national award: National Hotel Sales Manager of the Year.

When I learned I had been nominated, I also learned one of my competitors for the award was Marriot's Vice President of Sales, Bud Grice.

I was very grateful to my team for putting my name in the hat, but I thought Bud was a shoe in to win. At that time, he was "Mr. Hotel Sales," an industry icon.

When I received word that I had beat out the icon, and been named Hotel Sales Manager of the Year, I was shocked. I had a hard time finding the right words to express my gratitude for the incredible presentation and for the support I had received from everyone at the Century Plaza, Western International Hotels, and the convention industry.

My wonderful and very supportive spouse, Bobbie, and I spent an incredible weekend being hosted by the members of Sigma Iota at Washington State University (WSU) in Pullman, Washington. Sigma Iota was the WSU hotel honorary group that managed the Hotel Sales Manager of the Year award. Here I met Peter Smith, President of Sigma Iota, for the first time. Peter went on to become the very successful General Manager and Officer of Western (Westin) International Hotels.

It was a marvelous weekend. Being a Husky—a graduate of the University of Washington (UW)—in Cougar (WSU) country was a unique and wonderful experience. When I was asked to serve on WSU's School of Hospitality Business Management (HBM) advisory board thirty-three years later, it was a no-brainer.

I was deeply moved by the comments of those inside and outside the company who supported me in receiving this once-in-a-lifetime honor and would like to quote some of them here so you realize what an honor I felt it truly was:

"Not only is Dave a longtime and highly respected member of the professional team at the Century Plaza and Western International Hotels, but he has a strong sense of citizenship responsibility and a motivation that extends beyond his day-to-day activities."

— Eddie Carlson, Chairman & CEO,
Western Hotels International

"I can say without question that in my twenty-nine years in the hotel business, I have never met a man more qualified to be chosen National Hotel Salesman of the Year."

— Harry Mullikin, Vice President, Western International Hotels

"Dave Evans has shown the wisdom of selecting the right people for the right job to assist him in presenting the hotel he represents in the best possible posture."

— Bob Wood, CBS, Director of Affiliate Relations

"The finest attribute any hotel salesman can be noted for is a reputation for fulfilling commitments and f or making the best of any difficult or unpredictable situation. Mr. Evans can be commended on both counts."

— William S. Storey, CAE, Executive VP,
Institute of Scrap Iron and Steel

"We first met Dave Evans when he requested and received permission to make a presentation for the Century Plaza.... So impressed were our board members with his enthusiasm and thoroughness that they appointed a committee immediately following our meeting to look at the unfinished Century Plaza. Because of Dave's expert guidance, the committee for the first time ever booked a convention into an unfinished hotel, a move we have never had cause to regret."

— C.M. McMillan, Executive Vice President, National Candy Wholesalers Association (NCWA)

(NCWA met continuously at the CPH for ten years, until the exhibit got too large for a hotel.)

"He has displayed consistently a phenomenal knowledge of various aspects of the association business, and I must say above all else he has convinced me of the professional attitude of his hotel. I always feel confident about sending business to the Century Plaza. In my role at NAPA I have met many hotel salesmen. I do not hesitate to say that Mr. Evans ranks among highest caliber, if not the highest I have ever dealt with."

— John Gray Executive Director, National Asphalt Pavement Association

"He knits together five individual salesmen into a precision team— giving direction and, yes, allowing us to be individuals. If is not often in this industry that a director of sales can be an administrator and an excellent salesperson.... David is one of the few exceptions."

— The Century Plaza Sales Team, Bruce Lucker, Brian Drour, Jack O'Hara, Ron Snell, and Pat O'Daniel

"Join women's lib? Not, when a group of sales secretaries have a man like Mr. David Evans heading our jet-propelled sales department of

*female members. His department of well-organized productiveness has
made him the envy of others in the same field of endeavor."*

— Century Plaza Sales Secretaries Team: Jean Kappert (my secretary), Pat Simanski, Susan Pfister, Marie Mickelbart, Maggie Hope, Jean Robinson, and Charlene Chabin (office administrator)

The Los Angeles market was competitive and not a very desirable location for meetings. Smog and freeways had to be overcome. Las Vegas was very much a part of our group market "competitive set," I learned a lot during this time from Sig Front, Vice President of Sales at the Sahara, and Charlie Monahan, Vice President of Sales at Caesar's Palace. Both were very instrumental with my growth and development and helped me stay competitive.

The Century Plaza Hotel's number one competitor was the Beverly Hilton. Steve Sherrill was the director of sales there, and he was solidly entrenched in the Los Angeles market. Steve was the former president of the local Hotel Sales Management Association chapter, and although very gracious, he was a tough competitor. The Beverly Hilton was the centerpiece of Beverly Hills and the entertainment industry's social center. In addition, the Hilton's owner, Baron Hilton, was very active in the Los Angeles social world and entertainment industry.

I had my work cut out for me. My goal was to change the scene forever and make the Century Plaza Hotel the new entertainment and social center of Los Angeles, with our spectacular new property just a spit away from Beverly Hills, in Century City.

The Ambassador Hotel, with its world-famous Coconut Grove, was also a "celebrity hollow." The Biltmore was located in downtown Los Angeles and owned by a prominent local family. It was the centerpiece off all social activity in downtown Los Angeles.

Frank Widman, Vice President of Sales for the Ambassador, and Benny Gould, Vice President of Sales for the Biltmore, were fixtures in the Los Angeles area, each about twenty years my senior. Between them, they had about one hundred years of experience.

I was the new kid on the block in 1964 as CPH's sales manager, and the youngest director of sales of a major property in Southern California in 1966.

When I attended my first Southern California Hotel Sales Management Association meeting in Los Angeles, I had the sense I was a rookie on the block while the big boys stuck to themselves. (The association's membership ranged from Santa Barbara to Palm Springs and San Diego with 200 members.)

However, I was able to break through the glass ceiling in short order. I was welcomed to Los Angeles, when I moved the National Candy Wholesalers Association to the Century Plaza in 1967 after its long tenure at the Biltmore. At our next HSMA meeting, Benny Gould, Biltmore Vice President of Sales, was gracious about his defeat. He came up to me with his ever-present cigar in his mouth and said, "Welcome to Los Angeles, kid." I had finally arrived. After that, I was in the inner circle.

CS = PR² Lesson: There is a pot of gold at the end of the rainbow!

In 1968, Gene Autry, the famous cowboy actor, built a new hotel on the Sunset Strip. I received a call from his assistant, indicating he wanted to meet me for breakfast at his new hotel. Somewhat taken aback, but flattered, that this Hollywood celebrity wanted to meet with me, I accepted and met him for breakfast. I didn't know what he wanted, but I wasn't about to turn down a breakfast with the famous singing cowboy. Autry was very easy to talk to, and shortly after we got started that morning, I completely forgot who he was and saw him simply as a hotel owner and executive. He offered me a job as his director of sales. I had no interest in leaving CPH and graciously declined. We kept in touch, and although he had his own property, he loved the CPH.

CS = PR² Lesson: Don't be intimidated by title or celebrity status.
We all have feet of clay.

It's always easy to think the grass is greener somewhere else, and it would have been nice to say I worked for Gene Autry, but my gut instinct told me I was blessed with my position at the Century Plaza.

Here's a great common sense statement from world class hotel sales trainer Cindy Novotny on trusting your instincts:

> Trusting your gut instinct is also very important and the ability to just be simple with common sense. A few years ago, we were approached by someone who wanted us to work with them. Things about this person seemed a bit off "off." Common sense told me to run away and not look back. Well, I didn't use common sense and began to engage in developing a professional relationship with this person. The good news for me is that while my heart and soul was saying one thing—data was saying something else. Well the data began to fizzle and fall apart, and the common sense kicked in. Luckily for us, we disengaged before money was lost, relationships were hurt, and our reputation was tainted—I should have used my gut instincts and common sense right from the start.

CS = PR² Lesson: Stay on your chosen path, and don't let your
emotions get in the way of common sense. The grass is not
always greener on the other side.

Eventually, I learned not be intimidated by title or position. My parents had taught me that we all have feet of clay. Remembering this was very helpful in the complex world of Los Angeles.

As if the smog and freeways challenges Los Angeles faced weren't enough, we had to face the big guns in Las Vegas: venerable industry leader Sig Front, Vice President of Sales and Marketing at the

Sahara Hotel and President of the National HSMA, and Charlie Monahan, Vice President of Sales at Caesar's Palace. The Sahara Hotel and Caesar's Palace, along with the Dunes in Las Vegas, were our major competitors. Given the size of the Century Plaza's ballroom at 24,000 square feet (the Beverly Hilton's was 16,000), we faced Caesar's Palace and the Sahara often in getting business from conventions because of comparable size ballrooms.

I received a lesson in hotel sales from Charlie Monahan when a meeting planner who had just come from Caesar's Palace visited the Century Plaza for the first time. Our VIP practice was limited to a limo pickup at the airport escorted by the sales manager handling the account. We never came by freeway but took an alternate route through Culver City past MGM's large corner studio where *The Wizard of Oz* had been filmed, then up through the luxury residential area Cheviot Hills and smack into Twentieth Century Fox studios. This route eliminated the freeway perception of Los Angeles' freeways.

Having our VIPs see these two Hollywood movie behemoths firsthand—a type of entry down an Avenue of the Stars to reach the Century Plaza, was an eye-opener for our guests.

Then our VIP guest would be escorted to one of our large penthouse suites—the Presidential Suite if it were available—and we would have a nice fruit basket waiting. The fruit basket was standard fare then for VIPs at Western International Hotels.

Well, at Little Caesar's, the Sahara, and the Dunes, the fruit basket was long passé and had been replaced by the full bar setup.

So we discarded the fruit basket and replaced it with a full bar setup. I was admonished by our resident manager, Dan McClaskey, for this exorbitant expense. However, this new VIP amenity turned out to be less expensive than a fruit basket. The guest often only opened one bottle and left in the suite.

A tip of the hat to Caesar's Charlie Monahan for this sales lesson.

CS = PR² Lesson: Dare to change the status quo.

During the early days at WIH, we had no global office system to feed us leads. I had to improvise to create a "morphed" sales lead system, so we teamed with competitors, who shared many of the same groups alternating from the East to the West Coast. Those groups mirrored our group image at Miami Beach's five-star hotels, the Doral Hotel and the Fontainebleau Hotel.

So, my new best friends John Monahan, Vice President of Sales, at the Doral and Lou Rogers at the Fontainebleau became copartners in sharing group meeting leads. Both were nationally well-known as hotel sales superstars.

My lesson from Harry Mullikin to attend the international HSMA meetings to rub elbows with industry leaders was paying incredible dividends.

CS = PR² Lesson: Learn from the best in your chosen field.

In 1973, my career took an abrupt change when Harry Mullikin promoted me to Vice President of Western International Hotels headquarters in Seattle. At thirty-seven, I was the youngest vice president in Western International's history.

My new focus would be overseeing WIH Regional Sales Offices (RSO) around the globe.

My Canadian upbringing and my father's involvement with international buying had been a wonderful primer on international relations because I observed him work with all cultures and religious faiths. I would end up overseeing offices in London, Paris, Frankfurt, Toronto, Tokyo, Taipei, and Hong Kong, and later in 1999, when Westin Hotels and Resorts was purchased in 1998 from the Aoki Corporation, Sheraton Hotels and Resorts were added, so my global oversight list expanded to offices in Dubai, United Arab Emirates; Buenos Aires and Caracas in South America; and Sydney, Australia.

Harry Mullikin always encouraged all of us all to think outside the box. We did so with one RSO meetings held in Seattle. Through an unusual connection, we were able to conclude our meeting with a surprise visit to the *USS Nimitz,* the US Navy's oldest and finest aircraft carrier, whose home port was Bremerton, Washington. This was the first and last time any non-military group would meet aboard a US Navy ship.

CS = PR² Lesson: Dare to be different.

During my tenure, prior to the 1998 Starwood Merger, in addition to overseeing our global sales team and all global trade shows at Westin, I was frequently tapped to conduct new hotel marketing reviews. Simply stated, prior to Westin making the deal, I was to advise senior management and the Westin development team whether these proposed new hotels would "fly or not."

In the 1980s, Prince Hotels of Japan was owned by Japanese billionaire Yoshiaki Tsume. "Tsume-san" wanted to expand its sales presence into North America since Prince Hotels did not have any sales or brand presence in the Canada or United States yet. The head of our Japanese sales office, Akio Hirao, suggested to me that we go outside the box and include work with Prince Hotels along with our WIH hotels, since the US travel market to Japan was on the upswing and WIH had no presence in Japan.

We took on the North American marketing for the Prince group. Through our Japanese sales leader, Akio Hirao, we advised the Prince group with a pre- and post-opening North American marketing plan for the new Akasaka Prince Hotel in Tokyo and the new Takaragaike Prince Hotel in Kyoto.

We were very successful with our North American marketing efforts for the new Akasaka Hotel. This was due in no small part to our marketing partner, Seattle's Cole and Weber agency and its senior vice president, Jim McFarland. I challenged Jim to come up with something different since all hotels in Japan were selling to the North American traveler based on the popularity of the 1956 film *Tea House of the August Moon*. Jim came up with a brilliant program we called the "How to Japan Kit." It was geared to help the American businessman be successful doing business in Japan.

This marketing plan was so successful that the Akasaka Prince Hotel became number four in their market in the first year. Three hotels that beat it out, including the venerable Imperial Hotel, had been in the market since the 1930s.

We were so successful that Prince senior management asked us to do the same for the new Prince Takaragaike Hotel, still under construction in Kyoto. I was invited, along with Akio Hirao, to the all-Japanese Shinto blessing prior to the opening. I was the first and last non-Prince Hotel executive, a *gaijin* (foreigner), to attend such an event. It was an incredible, once-in-a-lifetime honor for me.

Despite my first thirty wonderful years with WIH, years of growth and development, my last ten years, saw the good ship *Westin* headed into stormy waters. This was a period of chaos, anxiety, and change. It reminded me of the last days of the Roman Empire when the emperors lasted months, not years. We changed owners three times and company presidents four times during this period.

In1999, CEO Harry Mullikin and Senior Vice President Finance John Calvert, who had only worked there a year, began trying to sell the company. In 2004, Westin was purchased by the Aoki Construction Company of Japan. The Aoki Construction Company's CEO, John Aoki, became Westin's CEO. His spouse Cheiko Aoki, the Executive Vice President, become my direct report. Both were based in Tokyo.

The Aokis didn't have a clue how to operate a hotel company, especially one in North America while managing it from Japan. Chaos and mismanagement was prevalent from the day they bought the company, causing the heart and soul of what was of a once proud and successful hotel management company to go out the window. In 2008, the Aokis sold Westin to Barry Sternlicht, a real estate entrepreneur and the founder of Starwood Hotels and Resorts.

During these Aoki years, I reported to the chairman's spouse, Mrs. Cheiko Aoki. She was a delightful person, who had once worked as a secretary in a travel agency in Sao Paulo. The chairman, John Aoki, had left his first wife and married Chieko while living in Brazil. John moved to Tokyo with his new spouse Cheiko to assume the leadership of Aoki Construction from his father the founder Masuji Aoki in 1978.

As an example of the chaos during this period, all expenses had to go through the Japanese "*Ringisho*" process, a very tedious and exasperating way to get bills approved and paid. All parties who had anything to do with this expense had to "chop" (stamp) the expense forms. We all had our signatures in a "Japanese character block," and we "chopped" (stamped) in the proper square on the expense form. In my case, my chop would go to the Senior Vice President of Finance, then to the Senior Vice President of Operations John Chin, then to my direct report Cheiko Aoki, and finally to CEO John Aoki. Since corporate HQ was now split between Seattle and Tokyo, this convoluted process meant it could take weeks to get my American Express approved.

To expedite the process, I made "chops" for all three executives between myself and Mrs. Aoki and sent the "chop approvals" directly to Mrs. Aoki.

This solution worked for the entire time I worked for Mrs. Aoki. Our office expenses were approved within days. *Let me make this clear—there was no intent to bury expenses, just to expedite the process, and it worked.*

CS = PR² Lesson: At times, you must think outside the box and use your initiative to fix a problem.

Over time, Westin ceased to exist as a hotel company. After years of success and innovation, many long-time Westin associates were fired for no reason other than poorly planned downsizing.

In 1998, we bought by Starwood Hotels and Resorts. I was promoted to Senior Vice President, reporting to President Fred Kleisner. My new job was to focus on industry relations, global sales, and marketing. During this time, the new Starwood Hotel and Resorts was attempting to become a new brand. I advised CEO Barry Sternlicht not to subordinate the Westin brand under Starwood Hotels and Resorts because the Westin brand was the premier brand in the upper upscale hotel market. Barry didn't listen.

This turned out to be a very bad move. The great seventy-year-old Westin brand, the leader in the upper upscale brand segment, went to sleep as a stand-alone premier hotel brand. Later, prior to my early retirement, when I met with Juergen Bartells, President of Starwood Hotels and Resorts, one on one in his office, he shocked me by saying, "We made a serious mistake with the Westin Brand." Two weeks later, Bartells had a spat with CEO Barry Sternlicht and resigned from Westin.

CS = PR² Lesson: Never subordinate a great brand.
— *Duane Knapp, Brand Strategy, Inc.*

Despite how my career ended, I took the right fork in the road in 1961 when I left KING-TV. Following the understanding that $CS = PR^2$ led me down the right path in my career journey, and I received my PhD in Life Smarts along the way. I was blessed to be in the right place in the right time and to have the common sense to know how to remain in that place. I hope this book will help the reader also learn to go the down the path of common sense.

"There may be luck in getting a job, but there is no luck in keeping it."
— J. Ogden Armour, Owner and President
of Armour & Company

CHAPTER ONE
WHAT I LEARNED IN MY CAREER TAKEAWAYS

- Turning your clients into friends is the formula for success.
- The art of selling is listening. Get to know your client. Curiosity may have killed the cat, but never a salesperson.
- Don't burn bridges. Today's challenge may be tomorrow's success.
- No risk, no gain
- Give your team members the tools and let them do their jobs.
- Over-plan in production by 10 percent and under-plan with your budget by 10 percent.
- Stay on your chosen path, and don't let your emotions get in the way of common sense. The grass is not always greener on the other side.
- Dare to change the status quo.
- "Never subordinate a great brand." — Duane Knapp, Brand Strategy, Inc.

What three or more lesson did you learn from this chapter?

1. _____

2. _____

3. _____

"The difference between a successful person and others is not a lack of strength but rather a lack of will."

— Vince Lombardi

2

LESSONS LEARNED FROM FAMILY AND FRIENDS

"Kindness is the benchmark for humanity."

— Dalai Lama

As I watch the world move into the high-speed "techie" realm and observe my oldest son Greg and daughter-in-law Lynn nearly exhausted between soccer, lacrosse, football, choir, and who knows what else, I often reflect on my youth and how unplanned our lives were back then. We functioned by our instincts. Simply stated, we were not managed 24/7; we had to think for ourselves and thus created a natural common sense.

Today, I observe so many cases where a simple common sense solution would suffice. Now things have become overly complicated by technology. This new world was supposed to make our lives simpler, but we have substituted machines for our common sense.

Now, we often don't know which way to turn for a common sense solution. We are so inundated with information from email, Facebook, LinkedIn, Google, Twitter, and the rest of the uncontrolled Social Media, that we overlook a simple $CS = PR^2$ solution to an issue or problem.

I learned my manners and the value of hard work at a very early age from my parents.

My father put me to work when I was thirteen in his company, the BC Collateral—at the time, the second largest jewelry and pawn shop in Canada.

My father, Alfred Abraham Evans, was Jewish and my mother, Katherine Elaine Hancox, was Anglican—Church of England. My dad's father, Harry Evans, was the patriarch of the Conservative Jewish Movement, and my mother's parents, George and Victoria Hancox, were patriarchs of the Anglican Church, in Vancouver, British Columbia.

As a result of this upbringing I became confused and questioned religion at a very early age. In later life, when I began reading and exploring other faiths, I developed a common sense approach to life

When I was ten, I was placed in Vancouver College, a Christian Brothers boarding school. To say it was a strict place is putting it mildly. At Vancouver College, I was introduced to Catholicism 24/7. To appease my dads' Jewish father, I prepared for a Bar Mitzvah while attending Vancouver College, even though, at the time, I was being brought up to celebrate Easter and Christmas. Consequently, I received an education in the Old and New Testaments at the same time!

The summer I reached the ripe old age of thirteen, my father put me to work at my first job—working half-days at BC Collateral doing odd jobs. The most interesting part of this experience was learning about people.

This business was located at 77 East Hastings, a block from Vancouver's renowned Chinatown, and next to a beer parlor. This beer parlor was the most barbaric drinking establishment known to man. British Columbia was dry at the time, so this bizarre place was one of the few where you could get a beer. Frequently, outside my dad's business were out-of-work loggers and other disadvantaged people, more often than not drunk from the nearby beer parlor.

This situation was overlooked by the police since being drunk was not an offense at the time, and tolerated in that part of town.

Despite his business' location, my father was an expert jeweler—one of the best in Canada. The BC Collateral played host to many prominent Vancouver citizens because of my mother's family connections. For example, her father, Judge George Hancox, was the Chief Justice of the British Columbia Supreme Court. These prominent locals came either to buy expensive jewelry, or to pawn, yes, pawn expensive jewelry for one reason or another. In any given moment, a drunken logger or a well-dressed man or woman of Vancouver's elite would come into the store and greet my dad with, "Hi, Alfie!"

So by age thirteen, I had experienced three religions and seen the world in a nutshell while working in the east end of Vancouver. This education, no doubt, gave me the insights and common sense to appreciate and understand different cultures and people's differences later in life. This understanding stood me in good stead when I was Western International's general sales manager and then a vice president and had management oversight for our global sales offices in Japan.

I worked every year after that. At fourteen, I spent my first full day working in my uncle's warehouse. When I was fifteen and sixteen, I worked for my cousin who owned a 7UP franchise from Winnipeg to Victoria. Working on the soda pop truck, delivering 7UP to the stores in West Vancouver, and enjoying an occasional glass of beer—one only—in the Canadian Legion (British Columbia's liquor laws were very liberal for private clubs), made this a wonderful job.

At seventeen, I entered the hotel business at Harrison Hot Springs Hotel, just sixty miles from Vancouver, and a classy getaway for Vancouver's elite and visiting Americans from Washington State. This hotel was well known for its healing, sulfur hot springs.

My first job at Harrison was cleaning slop in the employees' restroom. Then I moved to the front desk for a short spell. Then one of our long-term bellmen resigned. I was in the right place at the right time and became bellman #10. I kept that position for the rest of my "career" at Harrison, which spanned two summers and one Christmas vacation.

At the Harrison Resort, I learned a valuable lesson:

$CS = PR^2$ *Lesson: Don't judge a book by its cover; i.e., do not judge guests/customers by the cars they drive or how they dress.*

One Friday morning, a busy check-in day for weekend guests from the United States, which made up a good portion of our guest mix, my friend David Campbell, "Bellman" #9, and I noticed a beat-up Pontiac from Washington State coming to the hotel's front entrance.

David, who one day would rise to be the hotel's managing director, turned to me and said, "You take this. I'm going to get some breakfast." And so I did, and what a lesson I learned from that one opportunity. I sensed at the time that David didn't want to get "stiffed" (no tip), so he decided to step away but what a mistake he had just made.

I welcomed the couple, who were in their mid-50s, and took them and their baggage to their room, all the while expecting a very modest tip. We had been taught by our very tough general manager, Mason Nureck, "Never count your tips during the day and never look at the money when it is presented. Just look at the guest and say thank you."

After I was tipped, I thanked the guests and left the room. I had started back to the lobby when my curiosity got the best of me. Not heeding my boss's advice, I reached into my pocket and pulled out the bill the guest had given to me. To my shock, it was a whopping $5.00. Now this was in 1953. It would be about the equivalent of

$50 today. I thought the guest had made a mistake, but I was fearful of returning it because I might be reprimanded for anticipating tips, so I decided to leave well enough alone. However, the situation was only to get better.

The bell staff was responsible for delivering soft beverages and mixers to the guests. Because I had "roomed" this couple from Seattle, I was their bellman of choice to respond to their requests throughout the weekend. At the end of the weekend after they departed, I checked them out with their bags. They were very gracious, thanking me for my attentive service. The total of the gratuities for the weekend was another whopping number: $30.00.

Campbell was shocked when I told him. I had received a record tip for one bellman over one weekend—a record that wouldn't be broken for years.

I carried the valuable common sense lesson I had learned from this situation with me forever. I've learned people are not always who you perceive them to be so be very cautious in making quick judgments about them.

Given my confusing religious upbringing, this unusual experience taught me tolerance and understanding. Regardless of religion, people can be kind and good. Such experiences were great preparation for my future international work. I've also learned, thanks to Gordon Bass, President of Western International Hotels, "You can disagree, but don't be disagreeable." This statement applies to religion, politics, or any differences you may have with another person.

My family background and these early work experiences were invaluable for when I became part of the Century Plaza Hotel since Los Angeles was very diverse. Plus, our prime targets were people in the movie and TV industries, which included many Jewish executives, and by extension, Jewish social organizations.

Common sense in the hotel industry called for an understanding and a sensitivity to each culture and religion, and I had learned the CS = PR^2 of tolerance and understanding in my formative years.

Another valuable lesson I learned came from Eddie Carlson, CEO of Westin International Hotels. Today, the handwritten thank you note has been replaced with a text, email, or tweet. However, Eddie responded to every letter sent to him, more often than not, with a handwritten note. Today, if you want to shock someone you have met, or who has provided you with good service, send them a short, handwritten thank you note.

I think it's a serious mistake today not to teach young students basic handwriting skills. Perhaps I am being old-fashioned, but there is still something special about receiving a handwritten thank you note or at least a typed message via snail mail. Doing so shows that you truly care and have taken the time to show it rather than just banging off a quickie email. Given that technology has taken over the personal touch, such gestures of gratitude are even more meaningful today.

Nor do I believe good manners have been lost today. While writing this segment, I received a very thoughtful personal note from a respected hospitality consultant and former Westin Associate David Brudney (David Brudney and Associates, Carlsbad, CA). David was very aware, as a former Westin Associate, about my passion for sending handwritten thank you notes. With this note, received May 15, 2013, was included an extraordinary article David had taken from the *L.A. Times*. The article told the story of how superstar NFL Quarterback, Peyton Manning, writes personal thank you notes. Here is an extract from the article:

> Peyton Manning has had dozens of signature moments in his football career that the outside world didn't witness.
>
> Since childhood, Manning has jotted handwritten thank-you notes, and for years he has maintained a tradition of sending them to various NFL players retiring from the game....
>
> Manning said the habit of writing letters, as opposed to relying exclusively on email, is a holdover from childhood.

"My mother sent me an article one day on the fact that the handwritten letter was becoming a lost art in the text-messaging and email world," he said. "My mother writes handwritten letters...."

Manning went on to say that his mother wrote him a note in which she said, "if someone hosted you at their home, or [gave you] a wedding gift, or a thank-you gift, an email is not acceptable. A handwritten letter is what you must write." Manning gives his mother credit for his writing handwritten notes today.

When I was growing up in West Vancouver, my mother would always sit at Christmas time and write a personal note and add a "dainty hanky" to each of her lady friends. In all, she would send out some 300 Christmas Cards to family and friends. She would sit for hours thinking out each written note.

So often we say or think we are too busy to do the little things like express a simple "well done" to an associate.

I learned another valuable lesson about letter writing from my uncle which resonated for me throughout my career. In 1956, Prime Minister Winston Churchill retired from public service after more than sixty years. In April of that year my stepmother's brother, H. G. Scott, was living in Pender Island, British Columbia. He had served in the Canadian Army in both world wars and lived to tell about it. He sent Sir Winston a letter to thank him for his longtime service.

In keeping with his extraordinary communication style, Sir Winston sent my uncle a handwritten thank you note.

While visiting my father and stepmother one day, I was commiserating over my frustration in my efforts to have our Westin global sales team take the time to send out personal thank you notes.

My dad replied, "Let me show you something."

It was then I first saw these two incredible letters.

The Right Honourable Sir Winston Churchill KG., MP.,
House of Commons
London
England

HG Scott
"Ragusa"
North Pender Island
British Columbia
Canada
5 April 1959

Sir,

The radio this morning announced that you had gone to tender your resignation as Prime Minister to Her Majesty the Queen.

It must be an hour of deep regret at the laying down your work and at the same time of thankfulness that by your leadership in a time of the utmost danger you saved the freedom of Great Britain and the empire and the civilisation of the world.

I, who like many others had the honour to serve in the great wars and to see how Ypres was saved and Normandy won, beg to tender to you my abiding gratitude and thanks.

Ave atque vale

I have the honour to be
Sir,
Yours in the utmost respect

(H. G. Scott)

Note: The original is on Churchill's personal stationary with family crest. It is located in my safety deposit box at the Bank of America on Mercer Island, Washington.

This a copy of Winston Churchill's handwritten response.

Thank you so much for your kind message.
It gave me much pleasure.

Winston S Churchill
April 1955

My father let me take these incredible letters back to Seattle where I made copies of them and then put the originals away for safekeeping. Today, they are in my safe deposit box. I put the copies into a framed picture and hung them in my office. When I had visitors from our global regional and hotel sales teams and we were discussing sales protocols and my expectations for top rate performance and results, I would take them over to my Churchill handwritten note framed picture and say, "If you think you don't have the time to 'dare to be different' and display good manners with a timely handwritten thank you note, read this!

The Right Honourable Sir Winston Churchill,   Ragusa,
                              K.G., M.P.,   (North) Pender
     House of Commons,   British Columt
        London,   Canada,
          England.   5 April 1955.

Sir,
        The radio this morning announced that you had gone to 1
your resignation as Prime Minister to Her Majesty the Queer
        It must be an hour of deep regret at the laying down of
work and at the same time of thankfulness that by your lead
in a time of the utmost danger you saved the freedom of Gre
and the Empire and the civilisation of the world.
        I, who like so many others had the honour to serve in t
Wars and to see how Ypres was saved and Normandy was won, t
tender to you my abiding gratitude and thanks.
        Ave atque vale.

                    I have the honour to be,
                              Sir,
                    Yours with the utmost respect,

(H.G.Scott)

Thank you so much for your kind message. It gave me much pleasure.

Winston S. Churchill

April 29 55

I am very pleased to note "They got the picture!"

I have put my lessons learned from my mother, Peyton Manning and Sir Winston Churchill into practice by always taking the time to send personal thank you notes. I maintained this practice throughout my forty-year career and continue to do so in retirement.

Only in the last five years, due to arthritis challenges, have I occasionally typed a short note and included in one of my personal notecards.

And thanks to lessons learned from twenty-five years of work in Japan, I had "THANK YOU" printed on the reverse side of my business cards and added a small note with an appropriate saying for the recipient.

CS = PR² Lesson:
The handwritten note is a point of difference.

During my career, I was blessed to develop a long-lasting personal relationship with Roy B. Evans, President of the Professional Convention Management Association (PCMA), which was created in June 1982. Roy retired in 2000, leaving an incredible legacy. He was a master at creating relationships and a collaborative spirit between the supplier and meeting planner professions.

For years, the customer trade associations saw their relationship with the hospitality industry as very much a "we" and "they" relationship. I don't want to lead the reader to think these separate relationships were contentious, but there was a subtle barrier. For example, there was no representation on any industry boards from the supplier community. However, that changed when Roy B. Evans took over the helm of PCMA.

One of Roy's first objectives was to create a team relationship between supplier and planner, and he did so by convincing the PCMA board, in a very effective and collaborative way, of the value of having supplier members on the board. These new board members would be selected from the leadership of the hospitality industry and make PCMA a much more effective organization. This collaboration would allow the supplier side to gain valued insights into the association and corporate world and vice-versa. It transcended boundaries to help each element of the industry be more effective in their day-to-day jobs, allowing them to take better care of their client-friends-suppliers and better manage their individual functions within their organizations.

On his watch, Roy also created the PCMA foundation. This important industry-changing initiative was developed by a team of collaborative leaders. On the trade association side were Robert Hobart, VP of the American Medical Association; David Noonan,

Executive VP of the American Academy of Ophthalmology; and Bob Donovan, VP of the American Hospital Association. On the suppler side were James P. Evans, Vice President-Sales, Hyatt; Brian Steven, Vice President-Sales, Hilton; and David R. Evans, Vice President & General Sales Manager, Westin Hotels and Resorts.

Roy stepped way outside the box when he appointed me as the first supplier to the PCMA Executive Committee, and the same time as Brad Claxton, Executive VP of the American Academy of Dermatology was the elected Chair of PCMA. This very daring move made a supplier a member of the organization's inner circle— a first in the meeting-planning industry.

CS = PR² Lesson:
Creating a collaborative organization vs. a confrontational organization is just common sense.

CS = PR² Lesson: Partners get the job done.

Personally, I feel common sense is intuitive. Either you have it, or you don't. You can learn it and you can teach it.... In my management experience, I thought it made common sense to surround myself with people who were smarter than me. (Please, no comments on how easy this was.) Using common sense seemed to work with staff as well as those I dealt with on a business basis. It was as simple as that....

Twenty-five hundred years ago, the Chinese military philosopher Sun Tzu said, "If you know the enemy and you know yourself, you need not fear the result of a hundred battles."

By coming to understand each other in the workplace, we no longer have to be enemies. Instead, we collaborate and it becomes a much better situation for all in the long run.

*CS = PR² Lesson: Collaboration is better than confrontation.
You can catch more flies with honey than vinegar.*

Akio Hirao, a longtime Westin Associate, did an outstanding job managing Westin's sales office in Japan for over twenty-five years.

I began working with Akio when I assumed oversight of Westin's Tokyo office in 1974. In addition, I was responsible for overseeing and managing our Hotel Representation Agreements.

In Westin's early days, in order to expand the brand in Asia, Eddie Carlson, a pioneer CEO, created wonderful relationships with Asian hotel operators. So, it made a good deal of sense for Westin International Hotels to expand in Asia. However, at that time, WIH had very limited resources so Eddie convinced the owners of the Prince Hotel groups who owned Shangri-La Hotels to establish North American marketing and sales representation agreements to exchange reservations. This was an informal arrangement for some time with little to no direction or involvement by the WIH marketing division in Seattle.

In the 1980s, the Prince Hotel Group was owned by Japanese billionaire Yoshiaki Tsume. He wanted to expand the Prince brand in North America, with new properties on the horizon. Akio Hirao then suggested to me, "We need to step up our involvement since the US travel market to Japan is on the upswing."

I took on the North American marketing for the Prince group and Akio became the point person in Tokyo. On my watch, we advised the Prince Group on two wonderful new hotels to be developed, the Akasaka Prince Hotel in Tokyo and the Prince Takaragaike Hotel in Kyoto, with North American and post-opening sales and marketing plans. Prince Hotels was now officially part of the Westin family. It was "all ships steam ahead!"

When I visited our Japanese office, I had new mission: meet with the Prince Hotel Group's management teams for the Akasaka and Takanawa Prince Hotels. The Takaragaike Hotel in Kyoto was built later after the successful opening of the Akasaka Prince hotel.

During these often-challenging meetings with the Prince team, I was introduced to the most valuable CS = PR² lesson: "*Nemawashi*".

Nemawashi means "root binding." Plants and trees need all their roots working together in harmony to ensure their health. Similarly, all the roots of our organization needed to work together for it to be successful. In Japan, a small island where harmony is necessary, the roots are the people who must work together to achieve an objective. Confrontation is completely out of order. "The nail that stands up gets knocked down." Team work and cooperation are simply a way of life.

At our first Prince meeting, Akio advised me on how the conference table would be arranged for the representatives. Unlike a Western board table, where the chairperson or CEO sits at the head of the table, in Japan, the practice is for the senior person from each organization to sit across from each other in the middle of the table, therefore equalizing the positions with similar strength, thus beginning the *"Nemawashi"* (root binding) at the start of the proceedings. Discussions are then on an equal footing!

Root binding continued throughout my experiences. For example, I presented a new North American marketing program for the new Akasaka Prince Hotel at a review meeting. There was an open discussion and feedback to find out if there were any contentious issues in this proposed plan. We offered up a budget that was received with some concern over cost, but not content.

Then the next step of *nemawashi* took place. All parties leave with no decisions. It is now the responsibility of the associates, the number twos or threes, of the two organizations (in this case the Prince Group and the Westin Team) to hash out an agreement over lunch or dinner, with a beverage or two, in a non-contentious social atmosphere, where each party gets to know the other and can work out a proposal to be presented at the next *"Nemawashi"* meeting.

At the next meeting, the Prince Group senior person would offer an alternative or accept the plan. If there were remaining concerns, the second level *"Nemawashi"* meeting would take place again. This process would continue until consensus was reached on the proposed plan.

This may sound very conflated, but it works unlike the Westin way of taking it to the top, getting a flat "No!" and losing the day. I experienced *"Nemawashi"* first hand on many occasions in Japan, and I am pleased to report that Akio, Jim McFarland (principal manager of our advertising firm) and I were very successful in getting North American marketing programs underway. If we had used the Westin attack method, we would have failed.

It's said, "It takes six months to make a decision in Japan, but two minutes to implement it. In the United States, it takes two minutes to make a decision and six months to implement." Why the difference? Because in the United States, we don't build consensus during the negotiating process.

A collaborative (*nemawashi*) versus a confrontational approach can work in all cultures.

CS = PR² Lesson:
Teamwork on both sides of the table will improve results and profits.

I learned another valuable common sense lesson I'd like to share from David Noonan, Executive Vice President of the American Academy of Dermatology. David told me:

In the late '70s and early '80s, the accepted manner of registration for large medical meetings was the standard paper-based forms for either onsite or mail applications.

Physicians, with busy schedules, more often than not elected to use the onsite option. As a result, opening day registration lines stretched single file across the registration lobby, out the door, and down the street.

The idea of standing outdoors in Chicago on a cold November morning severely dampened attendee enthusiasm. Adding more staff and more registration counters did little to help attendees come in from the cold.

While watching a televised exhibition of the famed Le Mans Formula One auto race, the announcer described a solution chosen by the race managers to increase the race distance per lap without having to purchase even more of the French country-side. The Answer: A "chicane": An artificial narrowing or turn on a road or auto-racing course.

The twisting zig-zag pattern of the chicane provided more action turns (a crowd-pleaser), and lengthened the overall lap distance within an existing geographical footprint. It also packed more cars into a tight space!

Voila! By adopting a serpentine line system within the registration lobby, we solved a vexing issue and received favorable responses from the warm and dry attendees.

Common sense became the solution for this challenging registration issue.

CS = PR² Lesson: Get Creative when you are in a tough situation.

I learned a wonderful lesson from broadcasting legend Walter Cronkite on humility. Here is how it came about.

Late in my career in the mid-1990s, we were hosting the American Society of Travel Agents' (ASTA) board of directors at our Westin Pena Longa Hotel in Portugal. We partnered with American Express on this prestigious event. This wonderful hotel was owned by Cheiko Aoki, my current boss and executive vice president of Westin Hotels and Resorts.

Former US President George H. W. Bush was the keynote speaker at this event. President Bush was hosted by American Express CEO Kenneth Chenault and sat at his table.

At my table, Marsha Massey, our superb corporate tour and travel director, and I hosted Barbara Bush, the Ambassador to Portugal, her husband, and Walter Cronkite. Marsha was seated between Mrs. Bush and Walter Cronkite.

At the end of the dinner, Marsha came up to me. She said Walter Cronkite had a special request and wanted to speak with me.

I was stunned and asked her why.

"Just a moment," she said and brought Walter to meet me. I was taken aback by this and not sure what to say or do.

After saying what a pleasure it had been to meet him, I asked, "What can I do for your Walter?"

Now the shocker.

Walter told me one of his long-time wishes was to go to a University of Washington football game by boat. Here was the world's premiere broadcaster asking me to help him get to a football game. I felt humbled.

Walter Cronkite was recognized by many as the world's premiere broadcaster and a TV icon. He also had an eighty-foot boat on the Potomac—too far away to bring to a game in Washington, but all he wanted was to take a simple ride by boat to a University of Washington (UW) football game.

The University of Washington's football stadium is on beautiful Lake Washington. On game day, very big and very small yachts and boats are anchored to go the game. It's the best setting of any college football stadium in the country.

Marsha was aware of my UW alumni connections, many of whom had large boats, so she thought it would be no problem for me to set it up.

I asked Walter, "With all you have done and accomplished, why is this so important to you?"

"It is truly one of the most unique experiences in college sports," he replied, "so I always wanted to give it a go."

I replied, "This is the easiest request I've had in the last six months. No problem."

Unfortunately, Walter's boat ride never came to pass. He passed away before he could make it to Seattle.

Regardless, I was very moved and learned a valuable lesson in humility. We all have feet of clay. No matter what we have, often, it is the very simple things in life that we seek.

CS = PR² Lesson: Humility is the best mindset.
In reality, the simple things are what make us happy.

My Japanese *nemawashi* (root binding) lesson was instrumental in understanding that the objective was to build *shinyu* (trust). I learned a valuable *shinyu* lesson from a very busy person—NFL Commissioner, Pete Rozelle. He knew how to build trust and make time for everyone.

The NFL is big business for hotels and resorts, both for team stays and owners' meetings. The competition is fierce, so one must to build *shinyu* with the league owners and management to get anywhere. I was successful in establishing upfront a personal relationship with Pete Rozelle and his lovely wife Carrie. I had the good fortune to have him put his trust in me and the great team at the Century Plaza when we hosted the owners, NFL league management, and the players for the first NFC-AFC championship game in Los Angeles in 1967. All under one roof.

The name was changed the next year by Kansas City Chiefs owner Lamar Hunt to the Super Bowl.

I found out quickly that Pete, no matter how busy he was, had time for everyone, including a director of sales from the Century Plaza.

When I went to New York to make sales calls, the NFL was high on my list, but whether I had an appointment or not, the "Comish" (he was fondly called) would make time for me to visit him at his office.

We are all so busy in our careers today, especially with high-tech email, Facebook, and Twitter in the mix. That makes it easy to pass off those who may be deemed unimportant at the moment. However, as the famous proverb says, "You meet the same folks on the way down as on the way up." Commissioner Rozelle understood that and made it a point to treat everyone well.

CS = PR² Lesson: Make time for everyone;
you never know how it may impact your career.

Another lesson I learned while working on the NFL account was "If you can't fight 'em, join 'em!"

I learned this lesson from two very capable competitors, who became dear friends, Jim Jones and Sam Huff. Jim was Hyatt's sports teams sales executive, Sam was Marriott's sports executive and a former all-pro football player for the New York Giants. Both of these good competitors had very good relationships with Commissioner Rozelle.

The semi-annual owner's meetings was the crown jewel of group business in the hotel marketplace. This distinguished group of self-made millionaires and entrepreneurs met in luxury resorts and five-star city hotels. Because their business moved around, I decided to get to know my competitors as opposed to fighting them since the business would be shared by only a few resorts and select hotels. Between us, Westin, Hyatt, and Marriot had just "what the doctor ordered."

At one owner's meetings at a Hyatt, the three of us agreed to meet and share the business within our hotel groups. Hence the NFL owner's meetings rotated from the Marriott to the Hyatt to the Westin. This rotation remained in place at least until my retirement in 2000.

No, this was not antitrust. It was "creative sales"!

CS = PR² Lesson: If you can't fight them, join them,
or as August Busch said, "Making friends is our business,"
and that's true whether with a customer or a competitor!"

My insatiable curiosity held me in good stead when I was involved with the development of the Akasaka Prince Hotel in Tokyo.

The architect for this new hotel was Kenzo Tange. Tange was 5'2" and a world-renowned architect who was known for designing such buildings as the Peace Center in Hiroshima and the Supreme Court Building in Pakistan.

Tange created a very unusual lobby in the new Akasaka Prince Hotel completely void of any decorations, flower, or color; it was a sterile white—and not very appealing to the average guest when the hotel opened in 1996.

Since we were marketing to the North American business traveler, I was concerned this "operating room" look would not appeal to this market segment so we needed to add some color to the lobby. Therefore, I asked Akio Hirao to work with our Prince partner, Mideo Matsomoto, and Ken Kishi, Resident Manager, to make an appointment with Kenzo Tange.

When this incredible meeting came to pass, Akio and I met with Tange at his office, not far away in the Akasaka District. After learning more from him about his great work, we moved to discussing his design for the Akasaka Prince Hotel.

My curiosity went to work, so I asked him why the lobby didn't have decorations or flowers.

He was very gracious with his response. "David-san, when you are in the lobby of my hotel, you are the most important decoration. That should not be overseen by clutter and distractions."

I was stunned. This was the first time in my hotel work that any architect had given any consideration to the guest—what a unique concept.

This lesson was productive, and so was Tange's ability to be flexible. When I explained our position about the North American market, he agreed to put some colorful plants in the lobby.

CS = PR² Lesson: Curiosity may have killed the cat, but the right question at the right time can have very positive results.

Marketing the new Akasaka Prince Hotel in North America required a new approach to the North American Business and Leisure travel market. The marketing oversight assignment had many challenges and opportunities, notwithstanding how to overcome the traditional advertising that portrayed Tokyo and Japan as the home of *The Teahouse of the August Moon*, with geishas pouring tea in a tranquil environment.

I had the good fortune to have an outstanding, very creative member of our Westin marketing team, Jim McFarland, Vice President of Cole and Weber Advertising, to work with me on this exciting assignment.

Shortly before we opened this grand new hotel in the Akasaka District, I met with Jim in my office. There I had posted advertising for all the hotels in Tokyo, pointing out that they all had a *The Teahouse of the August Moon* theme. Then I told Jim, "We must be different."

Well, Jim came through in spades!

At that time, most American business models failed miserably in Japan because of their holier-than-thou "We have all the answers" mindset. So a plethora of organizations were trying to teach the Yanks how to do business in Japan with correct business protocols.

Jim came up with the idea to incorporate everything necessary to work successfully in Japan into a "How to Do Japan kit." We created a puzzle of the Akasaka Prince Hotel as part of the kit. Later, this puzzle was placed in the hotel's gift shop, and to our surprise, revenues from the puzzle paid for the whole promotion.

When we presented this idea to our Japanese counterparts, they loved the idea, so we went public with over 600 kits distributed in the United States. This not only won us the Public Relations Society's Best Promotion of the Year award, but we were very successful in capturing the attention of corporate America. We had put the Akasaka Prince Hotel at the forefront of Tokyo's major hotels.

In one year, the Akasaka Prince Hotel became number three in the market while the century-old Imperial Hotel was number one.

We succeeded because Jim McFarland, dared to be different when he presented this incredible marketing idea to me.

CS = PR² Lesson: Dare to be different.

I'd like to end this chapter with a few common sense comments from some wise men:
- "If you haven't grace, the Lord can give it to you. If you haven't learning, I'll help you to get it. But, if you haven't common sense, neither I, nor the Lord can give it to you." — John Brown of Haddington
- "One pound of learning requires ten pounds of common sense to apply it." — Persian Proverb
- "Common sense is the knack of seeing things as they are, and doing things as they ought to be done." — Calvin Ellis Stowe
- "Common sense is, of all kinds, even the most uncommon. It implies good judgment, sound discretion, and true and practical wisdom applied to common life." — Tryon Edwards

CS = PR² Lesson:
"Common Sense is a learned process that can become intuitive."
— Roy Evans, PCMA

CHAPTER TWO
LESSONS LEARNED FROM FRIENDS TAKEAWAYS

CS = PR² (Common Sense Equals Performance and Results Squared)

"Honor your parents.
Cultivate peaceful communities.
Be generous to the family.
Avoid anger and hostility.
Support schools and academies.
Work diligently in your chosen calling."

— Chinese Emperor Kangxi Maxims

- The handwritten note is the point of difference.
- A collaborative organization make common sense versus a confrontational organization.
- Partners get the job done.
- *Nemawashi* (root binding) works in all cultures. Common sense says "Teamwork on both sides of the table will improve results and profits."
- *Nemawashi* builds *shinyu* (trust).
- Get creative in tough situations.
- Humility is better than the alternative. More often than not, it is the very simple things that makes us happy.
- Never forget those who helped you up the ladder of success.
- Make time for everyone; you never know how it may impact on your career.
- If you can't fight them join them! "Making Friends is our business" (August Busch) with customers and competitors.

- Curiosity may have killed the cat; however, common sense says, "The right question at the right time can have very positive results."
- Dare to be different.
- Common sense is a learned process that can be intuitive.

What three or more lesson did you learn from this chapter?

1. _____

2. _____

3. _____

PART 2

COMMON SENSE LESSONS LEARNED IN SALES, MANAGEMENT AND LEADERSHIP

MANAGEMENT: The process of dealing with or controlling things or people. (Web Search)

LEADERDHIP: Establishing a clear vision; sharing that vision with others so that they will follow willingly; providing the information, knowledge, and methods to realize that vision; and coordinating and balancing the conflicting interests of all members and stakeholders.

A leader steps up in times of crisis and is able to think and act creatively in difficult situations. (Business Dictionary)

3

LESSONS IN MANAGEMENT

"We won't see eye to eye if we don't meet face to face."
— *Warren Buffett*

Wikipedia defines management as:

> Management in all business and organizational activities is the act of coordinating the efforts of people to accomplish desired goals and objectives using available resources efficiently and effectively. Management comprises planning, organizing, staffing, leading or directing, and controlling an organization (a group of one or more people or entities) or effort for the purpose of accomplishing a goal. Resourcing encompasses the deployment and manipulation of human resources, financial resources, technological resources, and natural resources.

> Since organizations can be viewed as systems, management can also be defined as human action, including design, to facilitate the production of useful outcomes from a system. This view opens the opportunity to "manage" oneself, a prerequisite to attempting to manage others.

TWO-MINUTE MANAGEMENT LESSONS

Why a two-minute management lesson? Because we all need some management continuing Education every once in a while.

LESSON ONE

An eagle was sitting on a tree resting, doing nothing. A small rabbit saw the eagle and asked him, "Can I also sit on my ass like you and do nothing?" The eagle answered, "Sure, why not." So, the rabbit sat on the ground below the eagle and rested. All of a sudden, a fox appeared, jumped on the rabbit and ate it.

Management Lesson: To be sitting on your posterior and doing nothing, you must be sitting very high up.

LESSON TWO

A turkey was chatting with a bull. "I would love to be able to get to the top of that tree," sighed the turkey, "but I haven't got the energy." "Well, why don't you nibble on some of my manure droppings?" replied the bull. "They're packed with nutrients." The turkey pecked at a lump of manure and found it gave him enough strength to reach the lowest branch of the tree. The next day, after eating some more dung, he reached the second branch. Finally, after a fourth night, he was proudly perched at the top of the tree. Soon he was promptly spotted by a farmer, who shot the turkey out of the tree.

Management Lesson: "BS" might get you to the top, but it won't keep you there.

LESSON THREE

A little bird was flying south for the winter. It was so cold the bird froze and fell to the ground in a large field. While it was lying there, a cow came by and dropped some dung on it. As the frozen bird lay there in the pile of cow dung, it began to realize how warm it was. The dung was thawing him out. He lay there all warm and happy and soon began to sing for joy. A passing cat heard the bird singing and came to investigate. Following the sound, the cat discovered the bird under the pile of cow dung and promptly dug him out and ate him.

Management Lessons:

1. When you're in deep "do-do", it's best to keep your mouth shut.

2. Not everyone who dumps on you is your enemy.

3. Not everyone who gets you out trouble is your friend.

This ends your two-minute management course.

In order, for you to engage your staff in providing the best service to your guests, clients, or partners, you must enroll them in your vision and align their perceptions and behaviors. You need to get them excited about where you are taking them while making sure they know what's in it for them.

Some of the common traits shared by strong managers are:

- **Being able to execute a vision:** Taking a strategic vision and breaking it down into a roadmap to be followed by the team.
- **An ability to direct day-to-day work efforts:** This involves reviewing resources needed and anticipating needs along the way.
- **Process management:** Establishing work rules, processes, standards, and operating procedures.
- **Being people-focused:** Looking after your people and their needs, listening to them, and involving them.

In order to engage your staff in providing the best service to your guests, clients, or partners, you must enroll them in your vision and align their perceptions and behaviors. You need to get then excited about where you are taking them, while making sure they know what is in it for them.

Good managers are people-focused and look after their associates and their needs. They listen to them and involve them in the decision-making process.

CS = PR² Lesson:
Get your team on board with vision for your goals and objectives.

"Most business problems require common sense rather than legal reference. They required good judgment and honesty of purpose."
— Edward N. Hurley, Federal Trade Commission

Here are two common sense lessons. The first is from renowned hospitality trainer Cindy Novotny:

Where common sense did not work has always been involving staff. My "gut" will tell me that I should fire someone on my team and I have continued to challenge my own common sense, only to be burned in the long run. Recently, a person who had worked for me for fifteen years started to show signs of problems. I ignored the obvious, I challenged my "gut thinking" and did not use common sense. In the long run, the person ended up going behind my back and selling our IP to a competitor under the table. Can I say I was shocked? No. My common sense knew there was trouble, but I ignored it. Never again. My best friend is named "Common Sense."

CS = PR² Lesson: When instincts tell you that you have problem,
take action. Any delays will only make it worse.

This next common sense lesson comes from Frank Gifford, former New York Giants player and broadcaster. It's a snippet from his book *The Greatest Game Ever.*

We said a prayer, of course. All the teams did. Father Dudley led the prayer—minus the robes and the cocktail condiments. Each time we prayed, I always remembered the time I went up to Father Dudley before a game and said, "Father, we're over here praying, and they're over there praying. How do you know who God favors?" "Frank, over the years," he said to me, "I have found that God seems to bless the team with the better personnel." Made sense to me.

CS = PR² Lesson: The best teams have the best players.

"It doesn't make sense to hire people and tell them what to do! We hired smart people, so they can tell us what to do."

— Steve Jobs

Warren Buffett has one of the best common sense lessons for all of us when solving an issue. Too often, we resort to text or email to communicate. This is the easy way out, and too often, this impersonal approach makes the matter worse. Buffett says, "We won't see eye to eye if we don't meet face to face." So be upfront and personal.

CS = PR² Lesson:
Good leaders face issues one-on- one with their associates.

My mantra has always been to have those whom everyone wants and who even want my job on my team.

We are all different, so don't expect those who work with you or report to you to all have the same "engine." Seek out their strengths and weaknesses.

Common sense prevails when we understand we are all different, marching to a different drum beat, with different interests and life goals. So often, strong managers will set standards based in their own work ethics and ambitions, often overlooking that their associates may achieve an organization's set goals and objectives but come at them in different and perhaps more productive ways.

Expecting all associates to march to the same drum is tantamount to failure and frustration for all parties involved.

CS = PR² Lesson: An effective manager recognizes people's strengths and weaknesses, builds on their strengths, and works on their weaknesses.

"Patience is a virtue." We are not all created equal. Associates come at problems in different ways. The good manager must understand this and take the time to build an interactive relationship. It is an important to get to know the "internal customer" (the associate) as it is to get to know the "external customer" (the buyer).

> *"Success cannot always be measured in dollars and cents*
> *but measured by the results achieved."*
> — George W. Bush, in his book *Decision Points*

Eddie Carlson, the revered leader of Westin International Hotels from 1959 to 1969 and then the CEO of United Airlines, was an incredible CEO and role model for a hands-on executive. Eddie started at the bottom and rose to be one of the most prominent leaders in all business. He did so by being a people-first person. In order to connect with his airline customer, he would often sit in coach to find out what the passenger liked or disliked. I don't recall any other airline CEO making such an effort to get to know a customer upfront and personal. Later, Bill Marriot took a page out of Eddie's playbook. He would become recognized for "managing by walking around."

Eddie was a no-nonsense, common-sense leader. His mantra was simple: "People make the difference." This became WIH's value proposition for years.

If Eddie met you, he never forgot you. He would be appalled today by some of the king-like CEOs who only remember the names of stock brokers, board members, and Wall Street analysts.

CS = PR² Lesson: Know thy associate and know thyself. We all march to a different drum so manage your associates' strengths and weaknesses.

Here are some common sense suggestions from David Gabri, CEO of Associated Luxury Hotels:

- An email or text cannot read the eyes nor feel the strength of a handshake when building a business relationship.
- Something always good happens when you meet face-to-face. So make it a practice to advance your success.
- Lead by example. It's simple enough, but regrettably most leaders fade from the front lines where they may be needed most.
- Lead by practical applications, not theoretical. So stay in the game to provide the best theory…and be prepared to test that again and again.
- In sales, use the Platinum Rule: Do unto others the way they want to be done unto to…. Sell them the way they want to buy (not the way you want to sell).
- In staffing, use the "Shaq" (Shaquille O'Neal) Plan. Put your best talent up against your competitor's best talent, region by region, or be prepared to be dunked on relentlessly. When Shaq was in the game, the opposing coaches had to align their teams differently, so understand your competition's talent and plan accordingly to win the game.

In my opinion, one of the best TV shows is *Undercover Boss*. It shows incredible examples of "management by walking around"—the management philosophy of Bill Marriott, founder of Marriott Hotels & Resorts. Marriott took a very modest, small company and turned it into a formable competitor on the world stage. He did so by getting to know his associates and listening to and learning from them. This is a leader/manager with class.

Jeff Senegal, retired CEO of Costco, was a champion of the associate and of hands-on store management. He would leave his comfortable headquarters in Issaquah, Washington to visit as many as six or seven Costco Warehouse stores in one day, listening to and learning from his associates.

These are leadership examples are often overlooked today by CEOs of companies with self-serving, tenured boards of directors, who are, more often than not, receiving nearly obscene levels of compensation. These king-like leaders are out of touch with day-to-day management, their internal (associates) and external customers.

The road is littered with bad leadership, resulting in corporate failures. The most recent example is Sears. Its CEO didn't have a clue what the brand was or who its customer was. Blaming online marketing and overlooking the proper positioning of the Sears' dominant brands, Kenmore Appliances and Craftsman tools, was a clear indication of how out of touch Sears' leadership was with reality.

There is nothing new in this book, only a reaffirmation human beings are blessed with the gift of reasoning, unlike animals, who are blessed with instincts. Unfortunately, we let our egos, emotions, and ambitions get in the way of common sense, thereby clouding good judgment and causing us to make uncalled-for mistakes.

CS = PR² Lesson: Don't lead/manage from the ivory tower.
You will be out of touch with reality and doomed for failure.

King-like leaders have always been out of touch. As Thomas Paine stated in *Common Sense*: "There is something exceedingly ridiculous on the composition of Monarchy, it first excludes a man [and woman] from means of information, yet empowers him to act in cases where the highest judgment is required." What was true of the kings in Paine's day is true of many CEOs today.

Good managers will see to it that their teams see them, when least expected, managing by walking around.

A common perception of sales associate in hotels is that they have nine to five jobs, and never work weekends, so when hotel salespeople show up at the least expected time—the Sunday opening reception, for example—they leave the impression of caring, and this further builds a strong bond with client.

CS = PR² Lesson: Dare to been seen, especially when it is least likely.

Long-time respected hotelier Steve Halliday, former Senior Vice President of Pan Pacific Hotels and former General Manager of Rosewood Hotel in Vancouver, BC, shares a wonderful common sense story from when he was manager of the Pan Pacific in Singapore.

MBWA (Managing by Walking Around)—Eddie Carlson taught me this very important management duty.

My first real job was as a dishwasher at a Vancouver icon restaurant called The White Spot in West Vancouver. Best hamburgers in the town. This group now is eighty-five years old. Washing dishes over two years, I became known as a pearl diver! My fellow dishwasher was named Charlie, a reformed alcoholic who showed me what hard work was all about. Those years formed my DNA for long hours and hard work and allowed me to appreciate what the service business was about—creating memories and happiness for your guests/customers. As you grow into a leader, you must focus on three things: people, product, and profit. Take care of your associates and have an outstanding product that meets what your guest is seeking and there will be profit.

The one key ingredient in the "people serving people" business is having *passion*. If you don't have it, get out fast....you will be wasting your valuable time. Be *firm*, but be very *fair*. Go places that people don't expect you to be in the hotel. Talk to your team and listen to their issues. Then most importantly, act upon them. Then monitor each action to ensure it gets done.

One day, three weeks after I had been transferred to an 800-room hotel in Singapore in 1995, I received a phone call from one of our team members. It was 9 a.m. on a Sunday, and I was just going to go golfing. The associate said, "One of our regular guests from India is in the Club Lounge having breakfast and said, 'Something feels different these days in the hotel...why?' The associate said that it was because I listened to the staff's concerns. The guest said, "Please call him. This is someone I must speak to and say congratulations to for making the hotel a better place." So I was called, and I went down to meet the guest. We became friends and still reach out to each other today. His name was Mr. Siva. Mr. Siva was a wealthy Indian businessman, a frequent guest at the hotel, who owned Sterling Communications, and he wanted to see the man who made everybody work at the hotel.

That's my quick story of common sense as I practice it 24/7.

CS = PR² Lesson: Do the unexpected and surprise your client/friend.

Here are some common sense rules from Andy Finn, former Westin Sales Associate and the current VP of Group Sales for Benchmark Hospitality:

The Golden Rule: Do unto others as you would have them do unto you.

The relationship the seller has with his/her customer, at its base level, is a "reciprocal" or "two-way" relationship (described in the Golden Rule) that involves both sides in a mutual fashion.

1. **Business Etiquette:** When you purchase items, do you appreciate it when the seller uses words like "Thank you," "Please," and "May I"? You probably do, so use those words with your own customer.

2. **Response Time:** Say you visit a Nordstrom. Unfortunately, they're out of the color of your favorite shirt. The salesperson does the required leg work and responds to you in a prompt manner. The shirt will be waiting for you at the store or it can be sent to your home address.

3. **Follow Up:** The sale has been made. The contract is signed. The customer, however, has asked for some specific information on destination management companies (DMCs) that it might consider using. The caring and conscientious salesperson takes the time to contact a DMC and follows up with a note, introducing the DMC to the client.

4. **Bad News:** Sales folks are exceptional at breaking good news, but not so much with the bad. The great ones prepare, visualize, consider alternatives, and fight (internally) for the right to do the right thing on behalf of the customer, and then they make the call. They don't "palm it off" on their supervisors. They make the call....

5. **Courtesy:** One of the (many) things my friend David Evans taught me is when you are leaving a voice message, do not leave the message as if you have a train to catch. Calmly and deliberately leave your telephone number (or email, address) not once but twice. Do it S-L-O-W-L-Y.

CS = PR^2 Lesson: Do unto others as you would have them do unto you!

It is important to let your associates know where they stand. The hardest thing for a manager to do is to be frank and upfront, but it's often necessary. That doesn't mean you should be an autocratic manager, just a fair one. In his book *Leading People*, Robert Rosen states:

> One of the biggest errors is to keep non-performers around for any reason. This inaction doesn't do any one associate or management any good. One must be fair and objective. The manager must move swiftly so as not to "poison the well" and if any manager thinks that his or her team is not aware, they have their heads in the sand.

Common sense suggests that it would be more beneficial to discuss the first concerns in a social environment (for example a rule against no alcohol at lunch). Unless it is a disciplinary event, which needs to be handled swiftly, in a business-like environment, a personal development issue is best handled in a constructive "soft" and "teaching" manner.

For example, address a concern quickly with a strongly worded warning. Detail the specific goals and timeline; for example, a ninety-day probation or cooling off period. Sometimes, employees may be oblivious to any problem, or they may be in denial, so your warning will be a wakeup call. As the supervisor, then meet with the employee at least once every thirty days to check on progress.

Cut the cord quickly for malfeasance. In all other situations, have in place a well-defined, constructive, and mutually agreed-upon plan for the associate's development. This fair approach will also get good vibes at the water cooler.

Whatever the enterprise, it is equally important to have a road map for success, aka a marketing/operations plan that is reviewed weekly by the director or manager responsible for achieving the approved goals and objectives. This road map is a moving target because in a free market society, markets, customers, and targets are very fluid and can change quickly. The chief marketing and sales officer (CMSO) in a hotel, for example, should sit in at these review meetings at the very least weekly, and in some dynamic commercial hotels, daily.

Manage to expectations by setting reasonable collaborative goals and objectives. My Starwood boss, President Fred Kleisner, left me with a simple common sense lesson: "What gets measure gets done"

In Chapter 9, I will outline the DREA (David R. Evans & Associates) process forms and guidelines for the "DREA Smart Plan Road Map for Success," which is an associate, operations team, and hotel owner friendly road map for an organization.

Mediocrity is perpetuated by process and micro-management. As Harry Mullikin, former CEO of Westin Hotels said, "Don't micro-manage or stifle your subordinates."

CS = PR² Lesson: Walk softly but carry a big stick. — Teddy Roosevelt

Here is a common sense example from former Westin President, Larry Magnan:

I have found that common sense is related to doing the right thing vs. doing things right. An example is when I attended an awards banquet at one of our Texas properties and was told that the banquet waitress who was serving our table should have been in attendance, but because her husband was a police officer who was wounded in the line of duty, she had to take a leave of absence to take care of him. As a result, she lost the seniority needed to attend and receive her pin. The GM and I am sure HR were doing things according the book, but I felt they were not doing the right thing. Common sense told her to stop serving and join our table, and I instructed the GM to reinstate her full seniority.

Another time, I was in Korea to close the deal to buy the three Chosen hotels from American Airlines. While I was there, the prime minister was assonated. The lawyers didn't want to go through with the deal, not knowing what would happen in the country. I convinced Harry we should, and the Koreans were very pleased, which helped show confidence to their people.

When the F&B corporate division requested more filling cabinets, I questioned the reasoning and learned they were requesting the hotel properties to generate reports that needed filing that corporate didn't need. When I questioned the common sense of this, I learned the hotels did not need them either and were only doing it for corporate!

CS = PR² Lesson: Do the right thing versus doing things right.

Another excellent example of common sense comes from Robert Brennan, CEO of Brennan Tours:

I would say that common sense played a role in everything we did.

When chartering motor coaches, we had very high standards. We expected our coach operators to maintain those same standards. "Going the extra mile was our mantra."

Here is an example of what we expected. When the coach arrived at the Seattle hotel and before we picked up our guests going on a Brennan tour, the escort would check the coach for cleanliness. First outside and then inside. On the outside, we checked the signage as well to make sure the luggage bins were clean. We checked that the drivers were washing equipment to clean the coach at the end of the day.

On the inside, we checked each seat to make sure it reclined and was secured. The bathrooms were checked to make sure they were clean and had adequate supplies.

The bins above the seats were checked to ensure they clean. This is one area where many coach companies fail. We'd have to get towels from the hotel and clean them on the spot before the guest arrived.

One would think that all these items would be standard operating procedures, but on more than one occasion, they weren't.

Once, motor coaches became aware of our common sense high standards, they got the picture and complied. They often passed on our common sense high standards to other coach companies so they would be prepared as well for a wonderful Brennan tour.

In many cases, they took it upon themselves to have dispatchers from each company make sure all items were covered and double-checked with each coach before it left the yard. "Getting things done with team work!"

As Robert Brennan describes, all that was needed here was "Management through Inclusion."

$CS = PR^2$ can be defined by the four elements of the acronym TEAM:

T = Together

E = Everyone

A = Achieves

M = Maximum Results

While writing this book, I was moved by a statement in an article in *USA Today* on May 29, 2013 that spoke to this idea of TEAM:

The Detroit Red Wings and the San Antonio spurs play in different sports in different leagues on different surfaces in different states, but make no mistake: They're the same team. Or, more to the point, they are the same organization—the gold standard of respective leagues for a generation.

I heard Peter O'Malley (owner LA Dodgers) say, "It is not realistic to believe that you are going to win every year, but you should approach ever year that way."

This is what these franchises have in common. They have committed owners who *let the people who are hired do their best.*

The February 2013 issue of Fortune's 100 Best Companies to Work For provided some excellent examples of hands-on management by leaders who had the best interests of the internal customer (associate and owner) and external customer (buyers) in mind.

#11 Qualcomm, San Diego: 15,963 Associates

"Employees...are encouraged to share ideas at an annual in-house tech conference. In 2012, engineers submitted nearly 200 papers. The winners were asked to present at the forum and participate in speaking events."

#17 REI, Kent, WA (Recreational Equipment):
10,767 Associates

"Paid sabbaticals come after 15 years with the company. Training for new hires includes an outdoor service project."

#27 Devon Energy Oklahoma City: 3,523 Associates

"Employees of this oil and gas producer value access to its senior executives. The President and CEO calls employees *or sends them a personalized note for a job well done* and regularly hosts employee luncheons."

#28 Kimpton Hotels & Restaurants, San Francisco:
7.480 Associates

"When workers at the boutique chain put in extra hours, the company sends flowers and gift baskets to their loved ones. It also hosts fireside chats with top executives. Associates at Kimpton, have been quoted as saying, 'We often lovingly joke about the "Kimpton Kool Aid," but it is more life blood. It's a phenomenon I have never see anywhere else.'"

#64 Marriott International, Bethesda, MD: 99,174 Associates

Ten of the employees have worked at Marriot for over twenty years.

#71 Whole Foods, Austin, TX: 64,127 Associates

The company is all about transparency. Employees can vote on new hires, go on field trips to meet suppliers, and are able to see everyone's salary.

#88 Nordstrom, Seattle, WA: 58,148 Associates

New employees, instead of a rule book, receive a note card that states: "Our one rule. Use good judgment in all situations."

More often than not today, CEOs' compensation is overstretched. Common sense goes out the window as CEOs become elitists in their own right, losing sight of the daily management of their companies. Instead, they set their sights on maintaining their high salaries, bonuses, and elegant lifestyles.

Control stifles innovation. Think of Adolf Hitler, Joseph Stalin, Fidel Castro, and Hugo Chavez. While they may have been efficient, any "cradle to grave" society or dictatorship stifles the human spirit and, thus, innovation. This type of overseeing government will last at the most for forty years (the life of the demagogue) until citizens have had enough and revolt.

Managers' most common mistake is to let their egos get in the way of common sense. By doing so, they create fear and stifle innovation. The road is littered with failures, as noted in a December 1, 2012 *Huffington Post* article titled "The Worst Business Decisions of All Time: 24/7 Wall St." The article relied on *Fortune* magazine's annual list of the 500 largest companies to identify those that lost the most money and made the worst decisions. Worst decisions were defined by companies who had made the list for ten consecutive years and then dropped off for good. Here are a few examples from the list:

DIGITAL EQUIPMENT

The fortunes of Digital Equipment, maker of minicomputers, began to decline in the 1990s. DEC, as the company was commonly known, had been successful because its products were less expensive than mainframe computers, which were made primarily by IBM (IBM). DEC controlled the minicomputer market from the mid-1960s until the early 1990s, but it failed to make a timely transition into the market for workstations and personal computers.

When DEC finally decided to get into PCs, it tried to use its own operating platform, VMS, though without success. Meanwhile, companies such as Hewlett-Packard (HPQ) and Sun Microsystems were able to gain market share in workstations by using the UNIX operating system, which allowed for many more software applications than VMS was able to handle.

Meanwhile, personal computers from Hewlett-Packard and IBM, which featured microprocessors and chip sets from Intel (INTC) and ran on Microsoft's (MSFT) operating system, began to dominate the PC market. (Microsoft publishes MSN Money.) DEC lost money every year from 1991 to 1996. The company was acquired by Compaq Computer in 1998. (Compaq was acquired by Hewlett-Packard in 2002).

KMART

Kmart's big mistake was made in the mid-to late 1990s, when management tried to compete with discount giant Wal-Mart Stores (WMT) on price.

Wal-Mart had the advantage of its "just-in-time" supply-chain system, which allowed the retailer to efficiently restock store shelves. Kmart failed to implement a similar system, which meant consumers became frustrated when its stores ran out of merchandise.

From June 1998 to June 2000, shares of Wal-Mart rose 82% as Kmart's stock fell by 63%.

New management was brought in to improve efficiency. But Kmart ran low on cash, and in 2002 it closed hundreds of stores and made a bankruptcy filing. Kmart merged with Sears, Roebuck in 2005.

AMERICAN MOTORS

By the time American Motors was absorbed by Chrysler, in 1987, the carmaker had been on a decline for more than two decades. The company's initial response to declining revenues was to expand its line of big cars, which carried larger profit margins.

American Motors bought the Jeep brand from Kaiser Jeep in 1970, but a weak economy hurt Jeep sales. With its cash flow slowed, American Motors struggled to respond to the threat from Japanese automakers, which were making inroads into the U.S. market with well-made, fuel-efficient vehicles. And, like other Detroit carmakers, American Motors operated under long-standing labor agreements that paid its employees more than Japanese workers were paid.

RCA (RADIO CORPORATION OF AMERICA)

Consumer electronics pioneer RCA—the first company to sell television sets to a wide market—was regarded as an innovator. You might say that in innovation lay the seeds of its demise.

Between the mid-1960s and the 1970s, it began to diversify beyond the scope of its traditional business. Its expansion was so rapid and so far-flung that the company became unmanageable. It bought a varied collection of companies, including publisher

Random House, in 1965, car rental company Hertz (HTZ), in 1967, and frozen-food maker Banquet, in 1970. The company even tried to make a push into IBM's (IBM) territory with mainframe computers.

As it diversified, RCA scaled back research-and-development spending in support of its core product lines. But when its acquisitions proved unsuccessful and RCA announced a return to its roots in TVs and other products, it had fallen behind lower-cost consumer electronics manufacturers from Asia.

EASTMAN KODAK

Eastman Kodak developed the digital camera in 1975 but did not invest in the technology for fear it would undercut sales of its film business.

Kodak's executives did not foresee the eventual decline of film. Only when consumers began to embrace digital photography, in the 1990s, did the company push into the digital market. But competitors such as Fuji (and Sony were controlling that market, and Kodak was unable to fully capitalize on the product it invented.

By 2010, it ranked sixth in the digital camera space, which by then was losing market share to smartphones and tablets. Eastman Kodak stock peaked in 1997 at more than $94 per share, proof that it often takes several years for poor decisions to destroy huge corporations. By 2011, the stock had dropped to 65 cents per share, and the company filed for bankruptcy.

CS = PR² Lesson: Winners are all made of same mojo. Mediocrity is perpetuated by process and micro-management.

Here are two examples of common sense from Larry Dustin, Westin Data systems management and operations consultant.

First example: Lesson from a Gifted Businessman with an Eighth Grade Education

I once worked for a wealthy businessman who owned a few hotel properties. On one occasion, his secretary notified me that the boss wanted to see me regarding the potential acquisition of small hotel chain located in the Midwest. Over lunch, (in his private dining room), the boss asked me what I thought about the chain.

Somewhat apologetically, I explained that I couldn't offer much in the way of specific advice, given that I had so little knowledge about the properties and the respective financial performance of each property. I remember explaining that without ADR (average daily rate) and occupancy information, it would be difficult to construct financial models from which to make judgments.

Although he listened to me with some patience, it was clear that he had a very different perspective and didn't give two hoots about ADR and occupancy. He then asked, "What is the largest property in the chain?" I replied, "Seven hundred rooms." He then asked what it would cost to build a 700-room hotel in that town. I replied, "At least $100,000 per room." The boss looked at me and said: "Isn't that $70,000,000?" I confirmed it was, and he said, "Hell, I can tender an offer to buy all the outstanding stock of the whole company for less than half the replacement cost of the one hotel."

He went on to explain there was additional value in the smaller properties that could be sold to further reduce his effective cost to acquire the chain.

Steeped in hotel jargon, I was until that day oblivious to the notion that one could "make money" in any way other than to increase revenues and decrease expenses. What the boss introduced to me was the whole notion of value and the importance of the balance sheet vs. income statement.

The boss was, for example, less focused on selling a $3.50 cocktail $3.50 and earning operating profit. What he wanted to do was buy the cocktail glass for $0.50 and sell it someday for $5.00. His view to earning money was all about buying and selling value. For him, the issue was always about assets and the value therein.

CS = PR² Lesson: There is more than one way to skin a cat.

Second example: Keeping It Simple

My boss, who ran a sizeable empire, enjoyed sitting behind a very large desk, slightly elevated from those who sat before him. He was constantly involved with numerous deals and had a modest staff of underlings visiting him constantly.

I always marveled at his clean desk, occupied only with a series of color-coded 3 x 5 cards, strategically located around his desk. He constantly referred to the cards during any conversation. There was nothing else on the desk except one pencil and one pen.

After years of working with him, and motivated by enormous curiosity, one day I managed to sneak a peek at the cards. To my amazement, each card was inscribed with just three questions:

What's the deal?

How much will this cost me?

What do I get?

No matter the deal or its complexity, every proposal submitted to the boss was subjected to the consistency of these three critically important questions and the brevity imposed by the dimensions of a 3 x 5 card. That's it. That's how the boss kept things simple.

By the way, did I mention that notwithstanding his eighth-grade education, my boss was a self-made multi-billionaire?

CS = PR² Lesson:
Keep it simple. Don't attempt to make a square out of a circle.

"A right judgment draws a profit from all things we see.
We cannot all be masters!"

— William Shakespeare

I once had the opportunity to address the University of Washington's Executive Masters Business Class. I challenged myself to prepare a simple model that addresses a chart for management success. I recently shared my Four Ps with the University of Washington President Anna Marie Cauce. She gave an "A" for this simple success formula.

DAVID R. EVANS & ASSOCIATES' (DREA'S)
FOUR Ps
P = PRODUCT
P = PEOPLE
P = PROCESS
P = PROFITS

- PRODUCT: Your product/brand
- PEOPLE = Associates, Stakeholders, Customers
- PROCESS = Analytics, systems and procedure
- PROFIT = The bottom line

The most effective manager will focus on the top two Ps: The system's "bottom line." History has validated this concept. Those managers/CEOs who take their eyes off the top two Ps to focus on the bottom two eventually join the ranks of failed companies.

"Mediocrity is perpetuated by process and micromanagement."

— Harry Mullikin, Westin CEO

As noted earlier, we are not created equal, so we all come at problems and solutions in different ways. A good CEO, division head or line man manager must understand that success is not always measured by dollars, the bottom line (the bottom P), but measured by results.

"He who is the ruler of men takes non-action as his way and considers impartiality as his treasure. He sits on the throne of non-action and rides upon the perfection of his officials."

— Tung Chung -Shu, 500 AD

"Once a decision was made, I didn't worry about it afterward."

— Harry Truman

Fast forward to Costco, another Washington State home-grown enterprise. Bloomberg, reporting in a June 10-16, 2013 issue reported: "While competitors lost customers to the internet and weathered a wave of investor pessimism, Costco's sales have grown 35% and stock price doubled since 2009."

CEO Craig Jelinek stated: "We know it's a lot more profitable in the long term to minimize employee turnover and maximize employee productivity, commitment and loyalty."

Costco's extraordinary success of Costco begins at the top with the business philosophy of its founders, Jim Senigal and Jeff Brotman. They believe in creating value, treating your employees and customers well, and respecting your vendors. They know what Westin Hotels also knew: People on all sides of the spectrum make the difference.

CS = PR² Lesson: All customers, internal and external, are to be treated with respect, dignity, and a smile.

Here is a common sense message from Don Freeman, CEO of Freeman Exhibit Decorating Company in Dallas, Texas:

Our business is built on relationships, yet no matter how close a friend you think you have, in a business relationship, you should never forget who the customer is.

Years ago, I had a call from a show manager, who introduced himself on the phone. Although I knew who he was, and our company had solicited the business, I was surprised when he asked if I would be interested in meeting with them since I knew our competitor really had a close relationship with them. In the meeting, which I attended with one of our salespeople, we both got the impression we had the business, and we had not even submitted a proposal. After we got the contract and did the show, I asked the customer what the decision process was. He simply said our competitor had forgotten who the customer was.

A few years after that, one of our good customers and a close friend really put us through the wringer on a bid process. I never knew if he was just pulling my chain, but remembering my experience mentioned above, I didn't take anything for granted. Maybe this is too obvious, but I have seen a lot of instances where relying too much on personal friendships sank the ship.

CS = PR² Lesson: Never forget who the customer is.

Nordstrom, a Fortune 100 employer, empowers its associates. According to *Fortune* magazine (February 20, 2013), in lieu of a rule book, the Nordstrom associate gets a notecard that says: "Our one rule: Use good judgment in all situations." Elmer Nordstrom, founder of the iconic retailer, set the stage for Nordstrom's extraordinary service by hiring associates willing to use instincts and good judgment. The company empowered them to do so without recourse.

According to John Metcalfe, founder and CEO of Associated Luxury Hotels, it is the little things that count when hiring people. John tells the following story:

I got a call from a hotel friend [competitor] saying she knew a bellman at her hotel who wanted to get into hotel sales. She also knew I was looking for an entry level salesperson. I told her to have him call me. He did and we set up an appointment for 10:00 a.m. on a Monday.

He showed up on time, we talked for about twenty minutes, and I really liked him. I told him to call me Wednesday at 10:15 a.m. And he did, exactly at 10:15. I told him to come back at 1:00 p.m. on Friday. He did, right on time. We spent half an hour together and I liked him even more. I told him I had one more candidate to interview and then I would make my decision. I told him to call me at 8:30 on Monday, and again, he did right on time.

We then set up an appointment for lunch on Wednesday, and it was there I hired him.

After each meeting, he sent me a thank you note for seeing him. Very impressive.

About three months later, we were at a reception and met a client we both knew. The client complimented me for hiring this man. I told him I liked him from the first ten minutes and knew right away he was the man for the job.

After the client left, my new hire asked me, "Boss, if you liked me at that first interview, why did you have me come back two more times?"

"You were a bellman, right?" I replied.

"Yes," he said.

"I just wanted to see how many suits you had!" I replied.

Incidentally, he went on to become area VP and managing director of a major resort in Hawaii.

Pick the best—those who want your job and those whom everyone else wants. The best executive, one with leadership skills and common sense, picks good associates to do what he wants to get done and has the self-restraint to keep from meddling with them while they do it.

> $CS = PR^2$ Lesson: The little things are what count when hiring
> associates. As Chester Nimitz, Five-Star Admiral in World
> War II, said, "Don't act quickly. Assess the situation."

Here's a common sense lesson from Jack Vaughn, legendary managing director of the Opryland Hotel and Resort in Nashville, on the need to be flexible.

Many, many years ago, while I was the number two executive at a large hotel in a major city, I gave the hotel's monetary Christmas thank-yous to the captains of the police, fire station, and post office for taking care of us through the year. It was tradition. I was meeting with my area VP that day when one of the clerks at the front desk came up and said the fire captain had been mistaken about how many gifts were needed for his men, and another $100 was required. I was about to leave the meeting to take care of the situation when the VP asked why I was leaving. After I told him, he said, "Oh, no, that's not the way." He told me what to do and then I went down to explain to the captain that we could not give him the extra $100. He said, "Fine, Jack. Wish the VP a very merry Christmas." The next day, a fire inspector stopped by to tell us we had to put in a movable fire wall in an area on our loading dock. Cost: $21,000.

CS = PR² Lesson:
A good leader is willing to look at all options and be flexible.

Shortly after I retired, I put together a list that, from my perspective, best describes a successful team of associates.

The 2006 Fortune 100 companies all had a common sense thread I identified in the DREA "characteristics of a good team." An autocratic top-down management may turn a quick profit, but any competitor who puts the two Ps (Product and People) first will win in the long run.

Characteristics of a good T.E.A.M.©

T = Together
E = Everyone
A = Achieves
M = Maximum Results

- Good Sense of Humor
- Minimal Distractions
- Honesty
- Respect
- Trust
- Tolerance
- Transparency
- Planning
- Good Communications
- Structure
- Tenacity
- A Sense of Urgency
- Accepting Others' Opinions
- Focus
- Leadership
- Ownership

COMMON TRAITS OF STRONG MANAGERS:

- **Ability to execute a vision:** Can take a strategic vision and break it down into a roadmap to be followed by the team.
- **Ability to direct:** Can direct day-to-day work efforts, review needed resources, and anticipate needs along the way.
- **Process Management:** Establishes work rules, processes, standards, and operating procedures
- **People Focused:** Looks after their people and their needs. Listens to them and involves them.

Micromanagement makes the *best people* quit! Brigette Hyacinth, author of *The Future of Leadership: Rise of Automation*, shares:

FIVE DAMAGING EFFECTS OF MICROMANAGEMENT

1. Decreased Productivity

2. Reduced Innovation

3. Lower Morale

4. High Staff Turnover

5. Loss of Trust

"The tree is known by its fruit."

— Matthew 12:33

CHAPTER THREE MANAGEMENT TAKEAWAYS

Management is a boots-on-the-ground, day-to-day tactical functioning activity that puts into action the organization's goals and objectives."

— David R. Evans

"I learned the easiest way for me to grow as person would be to surround myself with people much smarter than I am."

— Andy Rooney

"We won't see eye to eye if we don't meet face to face."

— Warren Buffett

- When instincts tell you that you have a problem, act. Any delays will only make it worse.
- The best teams have the best players. The little things are what count when hiring associates.
- "The man/woman who complains about the way the ball drops is likely the one who dropped the ball!" — Lou Holtz, legendary college football coach
- Pay peanuts and you get monkeys." — Keefer Welch, former Westin sales director.
- We all march to a different drum, so an effective manager recognize strengths and weaknesses, builds on the strengths, and works on the weaknesses. Don't manage from the ivory tower. You will be out of touch with reality and doomed for failure. Manage *up*, manage *down*, manage *out*. Be flexible!
- Pick the best—those who want your job and those whom everyone else wants.
- Do the unexpected and surprise your client/friend. Treat all customers, internal and external, with respect, dignity, and a smile.
- The Golden Rule: Do unto others as you would have them do unto you.

- Walk softly but carry a big stick.
- Do the right thing versus doing things right.
- "Hit a problem straight on." — Bob Tiffany, VP Equitable Life Insurance Company
- Bureaucracy and politics make for inefficient organizations. "Governments are a necessary evil." — Thomas Jefferson
- "The more technical we become, the more personal we must be." — Peter Drucker
- "Pay peanuts and you get monkeys." — Keefer Welch, former Westin sales director
- We all march to a different drum, so an effective manager recognize strengths and weaknesses, builds on the strengths, and works on the weaknesses.
- The little things are what count when hiring associates.
- "Don't act quickly. Assess the situation." — World War II Admiral Chester Nimitz
- Be flexible
- Don't manage from the ivory tower. You will be out of touch with reality and doomed for failure. Manage *up*, manage *down*, manage *out*.
- Do the unexpected and surprise your client/friend.
- The Golden Rule: Do unto others as you would have them do unto you.
- Walk softly, but carry a big stick.
- Do the right thing versus doing things right.
- "What gets measured gets done." — Fred Kleisner, former Westin President
- "The man/woman who complains about the way the ball drops is likely the one who dropped the ball!" — Lou Holtz, legendary college football coach
- There is more than one way to skin a cat.
- Keep it simple. Don't attempt to make a square out of a circle.

- Treat all customers, internal and external, with respect, dignity, and a smile.
- Never forget who the customer is. Associates, stockholders, and buyers are all stakeholders.
- Dare to be different. Think outside the box.
- Listen to your instincts. To do otherwise is tantamount to failure.
- "Practice management by walking around." — Bill Marriott, CEO of Marriott
- Patience. We are not all created equal. Associates come at problems in different ways. The good manager must understand this.
- "Inspect what you expect." — Fred Kleisner, Starwood President
- Don't cut your way to profits.
- "Hit a problem straight on." — Bob Tiffany, VP Equitable Life Insurance Company
- Pick the best—those who want your job and those whom everyone else wants. The best executive is the one who has the good common sense to pick good associates to do what he wants to get done, and the self-restraint to keep from meddling with them while they do it.
- Bureaucracy and politics make for inefficient organizations. "Governments are a necessary evil." — Thomas Jefferson

"The more technical we become, the more personal we must be."

— Peter Drucker

What three or more lessons did you learn in this chapter?

1. _____

2. _____

3. _____

4

LEADERSHIP

*"Wise men profit more from fools than fools from wise men,
for the wise man shuns the mistakes of fools, but fools
do not imitate the successes of the wise."*

— Cato the Elder

According to Wikipedia, leadership has been described as "a process of social influence in which one person can enlist the aid and support of others in the accomplishment of a common task." Other in-depth definitions of leadership have also emerged, including "Organizing a group of people to achieve a common goal." Leadership does not always require the leader to have formal authority. A leader is simply someone people follow for reasons that may involve the leader's traits, situational interaction, function, behavior, power, vision and values, charisma, and intelligence.

UNDERSTANDING THE DIFFERENCES: LEADERSHIP VS. MANAGEMENT

The main difference between leaders and managers is leaders have people who follow them while managers have people who work for them.

Successful business owners need to be both strong leaders and managers to get their teams on board to follow them toward their visions of success. Leadership is about getting people to understand your vision, believe in it, and work with you to achieve your goals. Managing is more about administering and making sure the day-to-day things are happening as they should.

While many traits make up a strong leader, some of the key characteristics, according to the British Columbia Tourism Commission, are:

- **Honesty & Integrity:** Honesty and integrity are crucial to get your people to believe you and buy in to the journey you are taking them on.
- **Vision:** Know where you are, where you want to go, and enroll your team in charting a path for the future.
- **Inspiration:** Inspire your team to be all they can by making sure they understand their role in the bigger picture.
- **Ability to Challenge:** Do not be afraid to challenge the status quo, do things differently, and have the courage to think outside the box
- **Communication Skills:** Keep your team informed of the journey, where you are, where you are heading, and share any roadblocks you may encounter along the way.

With smaller organizations, the challenge lies in making sure you are both leading your team and managing your day-to-day operation. Those able to do both will create a competitive advantage. Are you both a leader and a manager? What would your staff say if you were to ask them?

Whether or not you agree with George W. Bush's politics, this excerpt from his book *Decision Points* is an excellent example of a common sense approach to sound leadership and management:

> My goal was to assemble a team of talented people whose experience and skills complemented each other's and to whom I felt comfortable delegating. I wanted people who agreed on the direction of the administration but felt free to express differences on any issue. An important part of my job was to create a culture that encouraged teamwork and fostered loyalty not to me but to our country and our ideals.

Clyde Harris former Westin Associate and Holiday development executive shares the following common sense leadership lesson:

> After working for large companies within the hospitality industry for my entire career, it came time to broaden my reach and develop my own hospitality company, at a relatively late period in my life. Putting together the business plan, investors, and lenders was actually the easy portion of my task.

> Hiring people was a far more difficult and challenging assignment. Did I want seasoned pros who might be stuck in their ways, or did I want the younger, more aggressive team that could be molded, trained, and motivated properly?

> Well, I took the second route and was able to attract a young band of renegades who were smart, could be trained quickly, and had 100 percent buy-in of the objectives our young company was trying to accomplish.

> Over time, it became clear we clearly had to define our mantra to the line associates—to create a clear and concise message all could understand and believe in. Through my training and tutelage from some of the best leaders (including my former boss David Evans) within our industry, we developed the following as our company mantra:

Make and keep the customer happy through great service. Keep employee satisfaction and morale high, and those infamous net profits will automatically show up.

I might add that high employee satisfaction was not achieved by overpaying our associates; it was achieved by creating a team of focused associates who understood the assignment, had the tools to do the job, and were left alone to accomplish their task. Pretty simple, but it sure worked!

CS = PR² Lesson: High customer satisfaction plus high employee satisfaction is CS = PR². This simple formula equals higher net profits.

It's that simple.

The fundamental building block of leadership is $CS = PR^2$. When we substitute process and leave out $CS = PR^2$, we are doomed to failure.

The best leader is the one who has sense enough to pick good men and women to do what he wants and self-restraint enough to keep from meddling with them while they do it. When Jamie Dimon, CEO of JP Morgan, was asked "What do you look for in your leadership team?" his reply was: "Credibility, character, and how they treat people."

Following is a common sense story from Sig Front, the former Senior VP Sheraton Hotels and Resorts Sales and Marketing. He shares his experience of a great leader who is willing to step outside the box and develop his associates.

When I became a salesman for Schine Hotels, headquartered in Miami Beach, Will Coffman, who was the GM of Schine's downtown Miami hotel, took me by the hand and walked me through hundreds of techniques for surfacing prospects, contacting them, and creating an effective image with prospects before they even become interested in your property. Will would also drill me a lot on hotel operations and why it was so important to deliver what you promise to the individual or group. He made no bones about the need to be dedicated and give guests more than they want.

A leader's ability to develop new ideas and ask for people's help in implementing them may seem a common sense key to success. But the sad fact is, all too often, many of today's leaders resign themselves to limits imposed on them by flawed systems rather than rethinking those systems.

$$CS = PR^2:$$
Great leaders are great teachers who are willing to see outside the box.

There is judgmental and nonjudgmental controlling, and then there is relinquishing control. Many leaders are over-controlling and force their will on others (think Stalin, Henry VIII, Hitler, and Napoleon). This behavior leads to low morale, risk, a divided culture, and, ultimately, failure. They make snap decisions, without the facts, relying on their emotions and beliefs and ignoring the people around them. They are eager to criticize others to elevate themselves. On the other hand, great leaders use common sense to see things in an open, clear, non-judgmental manner. They examine all sides of a decision.

Doug Ducate, CEO of the Center of Exhibition Industry Research, shares an excellent example of common sense leadership, which can be summed up as "If your instincts say do it, do it!"

One of the best examples of effective, common sense leadership ever concerned the invasion of Normandy during World War II.

As you know, the allied forces were staged in the UK, battle-ready. Weather turned against them and they just had to sit and wait. Eisenhower knew he could not keep them at battle-ready forever, so when he got the slightest break in the weather, he ordered the assault.

They divided Normandy into five beaches: Juno, Gold, Omaha, Utah, and Sword. The plan was to attack from the north and hit the beaches in two waves. Allied forces were assigned different beaches. The US got Omaha and Utah.

Allied commanders were on ships in the English Channel. They were to relay to Eisenhower what was happening and to make battle decisions. The first thing that happened was a fog settled in, so they could not see the beaches. The second thing was they lost key radio contact with the landing forces, so they were basically without information. The reports they did have were of heavy fire and terrible casualties at Omaha.

The commanders on the ship disagreed about sending the second wave and they almost didn't send it. Historians agree if they had not sent the second wave, Big Red 1, leading the amphibious assault forces, would never have gotten off Omaha Beach and the day would have been lost.

The point is faced with a life-and-death decision concerning thousands of men, information and the lack of information told the commanders not to send the second wave...to play it safe. Instinct and experience told them if they didn't, the day was lost. They made the right decision—perhaps the most important decision in the war, and even in the century. One can only speculate what a huge defeat at Normandy would have done to the war effort.

CS = PR² Lesson: When your instincts say do it, do it!

"Seize the initiative and never relinquish it."

— Abraham Lincoln

CS = PR² ELEMENTS OF LEADERSHIP

Let's now look at some common sense elements of leadership.

1. **Doing what is right versus doing the right thing:** As leaders rise to the top, they can feel invincible and able to do anything they want. But great leaders have principles and follow them (think of Churchill, Truman, Lincoln, and Lee Iacocca, CEO of Chrysler). They choose convictions over desires, will over emotions, and clear thinking and self-control over the easy way out.

2. **Knowing it all versus being open to learning:** Not understanding or paying attention to history is a guarantee to repeat it, with failure. No leader knows everything. That is why the learning process never ends. Common sense says the learning curve has no end. "Stop, look, and listen" are the benchmarks for building relationships. The more open to learning the organization and its leaders are, the less susceptible they are to failure and outright disasters.

3. **Holding versus letting go:** Although at times it is necessary and even admirable for leaders to stick to their goals and hold to their course, they must also face reality and let go of what the organization needs. A common sense example comes from branding guru Duane Knapp, founder of Brand Strategy, Inc.: "Never subordinate a dominant brand."

   When Starwood bought Westin Hotels in the mid-'90s, Westin was the dominant brand in the upper upper-scale hotel market. Starwood leadership decided the new Starwood Hotels and Resorts (SH&R) would be the *brand de jour*, thereby placing the very successful Westin brand second.

   In a very short while, Westin went off the radar screen. Only a couple of years later did Sue Brush, Senior Vice President of Public Relations at Starwood Hotels & Resorts and a former Westin Heritage person, make a conscientious marketing effort to bring this great brand back into prominence. However, while Westin did get back into the mainstream, it never reacquired the dominant position it had enjoyed in the marketplace before this fateful decision.

The Starwood leadership overlooked common sense branding in spades!

4. **Impatient versus patient:** Many managers are impatient. They push too hard and overschedule associates. But common sense says you will achieve greater success if you can be patient and flexible, aiming for small successes in a short period of time, encouraging initiative, and gaining greater group buy-in.

   Patience was the order of the day during World War II in the Pacific. MacArthur and Nimitz had to live with the decision that the focus would be on defeating Hitler in Europe, so they decided patience was the order of the day and decided to bypass Japanese strongholds and island hop until the Allies' full forces could come to bear on the Pacific Front in May 1945.

   As Chinese military strategist Sun Tzu said 2,500 year ago: "The highest form of generalship is to balk the enemy's plans. The next best is to prevent the junction of the enemy's forces. The next is to attack the enemy. And the worst thing is to besiege walled cities. The general unable to control his irritation, will launch his men to the assault like swarming ants."

5. **Closed and defensive versus non-defensive:** Defensiveness compounds mistakes. We make an error, then dig in our heels. The ego-driven defensive leader builds interpersonal walls and can even generate turf wars. To avoid this, common sense says leaders must be open-minded, maintain a broad frame of references, and adapt themselves to people, processes, and situations.

   In the later days of World War II, Adolf Hitler, whose ego dictated his leadership and decisions, did not listen to his generals at the famed Battle of the Bulge where he faced overwhelming odds against the Allied Army of Americans, Australians, Brits, Canadians, and New Zealanders. (Hitler never read Sun Tzu.) His commanding general, von Rundstedt, stated, "I am not sure whether the pressure from behind is worse than from in front."

CS = PR² Lesson: Listen, listen, listen, and be flexible.

6. **Self-focused vs. team-focused:** Some leaders see themselves in everything they do. Great leaders value everyone, see reality with clarity, and base their decisions on what is happening, not what they wish was happening.

7. **Bad news does not go away, act quickly and decisively:** Here's An extract, from a May 2013 Bloomberg article by Claire Suddath that exemplifies the CS = PR² approach to giving bad news.

   "The key to keeping bad news constructive," says George Bradt, Managing Director, Prime Genesis, "is pre-emptive damage control. There are associates who are going to be very emotionally affected by what you are about to do. You can't let them find out this along with everyone else."

   CS = PR² suggests speaking to those employees no more than twenty-four hours before any announcement. Afterwards, the manager should encourage associates to come forward and talk to them.

   Shortly after I was promoted to Director of Sales at the Century Plaza Hotel in June 1966, I conducted comprehensive reviews of all the group meetings on the books. The company guideline at the time was that a group room block was ten or more rooms.

   In my first six months in my new position as Director of Sales at the Century Plaza Hotel, I had almost 100 percent turnover on my team through attrition and termination. I had to build a new team because I wanted to be sure all the business on the books was legitimate group business. I terminated one sales manager for bogus bookings.

To my shock, I found a serious error on the books. Our Century Plaza financial owner was The Equitable Life Insurance Company. We had a block of 450 rooms for its planned meeting in January 1967. I noted the block should have been 500, so we were fifty short.

I found this error in October 1966, so we now only had ninety days before Equitable was due to arrive, and worse, we had a small group booked at the same time.

Not a very good way to start my career as Director of Sales.

I decided to move quickly. The next day, at 6 a.m. I called Bob Tiffany, Equitable VP from my home. I will never forget Bob's response to my early morning call. "David, what time is it?" I told him, "Six a.m." He was surprised, but doing so helped to soften the blow since a call that early usually is a forewarning that something is wrong.

I told Bob the problem and that I would be coming to New York (from LA) tomorrow to work out the solution.

Fortunately, Bob and I worked things out. We did have to re-locate some of the meeting (thirty out of 450 attendees), but we had a plan in place so there were no surprises during the meeting.

What was most gratifying about this experience was that Bob Tiffany and I became great friends, booking many more Equitable meetings at the Century Plaza. And to my pleasant surprise, Bob shared this experience in the industry for years, as an excellent example of how to solve a problem quickly, with very positive long-term results.

A near disaster turned into a major positive!

*CS = PR² Lesson: Take care of bad news quickly because it
isn't going away. Do it fast, and with concern and
an appreciation for its recipient.*

8. **Be a good boss:** Here is another common sense leadership
    lesson from Clyde Harris, former Westin Associate, who over-
    saw Westin's sales office in New York, and former Holiday Inn
    development officer. It exemplifies what makes a good boss.

    Have you ever sat back and thought through the question
    of what makes a great boss? In my opinion, there are at least
    two types. Type 1 manages the P&L (profit & loss) and not
    his people. He is totally driven to produce the best NOI
    (net operating income) possible, while caring nothing about
    his staff, their development, nor their personal feelings. This
    type of person might be successful in the short term, but he
    will always fail in the long term. Why? Because people make
    the difference in a successful operation and will drive profits
    naturally, without being intimidated, bullied, or pushed for
    no apparent reason.

    Now the type 2 manager is the person I love. He is more
    than a manager; he is a leader. Take, for example, the three
    best leaders (managers) I had the pleasure to work with.
    The first, was my boss, David Evans, followed by Hermann
    Gammeter, both with Westin Hotels & Resorts; next came
    Steve Porter, President of InterContinental Hotels and
    Resorts.

    What made them so special was a common element they
    men shared. They clearly communicated the objective, made
    certain all staff members were clear on that objective, gave
    all staff the tools to complete the objective, let them attain
    the objective through their own ingenuity and creativity,
    and shared their success with much excitement. On the

other hand, if a staff member failed the assignment, given the above tools, there were justified ramifications to follow.

So, let's quickly review the difference between a manager and a leader. Manager might be successful in the short term, but they can also fail in the long term. Why? Because they have no buy in from their staffs, and eventually, their staffs could care less about the managers' goals. On the other hand, leaders develop teams that have 100 percent buy in of the objectives and accomplishes their objectives collectively, while enjoying their work environments.

Now which do you want to be?

9. **Make good decisions.**

*"You can't make good decisions unless you have good information
and can separate facts from opinion and speculation."*

— General Colin Powell

General Powell offered some common sense leadership and management lessons in the May 13, 2012 issue of *Newsweek* in "Colin Powell on the Bush Administration's Iraq War Mistakes." Here are some excerpts from that article:

> Over time I developed for my intelligence staffs a set of four rules to ensure we saw the process from the same perspective and to take off their shoulders some of the burdens of accountability:
>
> Tell me what you know.
>
> Tell me what you don't know.
>
> Tell me what you think.
>
> Always distinguish which is which.

What you know means you are reasonably sure your facts are corroborated. At best you know where they came from, and you confirm them with multiple sources....

What you don't know is just as important. There is nothing worse than a leader believing he has accurate information when folks who know he doesn't, don't tell him he doesn't. I have gotten into trouble when people who should have spoken up didn't....

Tell me what you think. Though verified facts are the golden nuggets of decision-making, unverified information, hunches, and even wild beliefs may sometimes prove to be just as important....

Always distinguish which is which. I want as many inputs as time, staff, and circumstances allow. I weigh them all—corroborated facts, analysis, opinions, hunches, informed instinct—and come up with a course of action....

10. **Resistance vs. Acceptance:** Great Leaders accept current reality, changing what they can and adapting to what they can't (think MacArthur and Nimitz in the Pacific War, Churchill opening a second front in Italy during World War II). A good leader is like a sports figure who accepts the situation on the playing field and deals with it. For example, when confronted by the power play in hockey, where one team has a player advantage, a good team leader will ensure that this advantage turns into a goal.

One reasons the Japanese lost World War II was their commanders' inflexibility. Contrary to World War II propaganda, Japan had some good generals, but their rigid Samurai culture didn't allow them to make changes on the spot or communicate with the other services. The Japanese Army did not talk directly to the Imperial Navy but had to go through High Command in Tokyo.

Here's a classic example: The well-respected Japanese Admiral Kurita at the 1944 Battle of Leyte Gulf in the Philippines faced overwhelming odds. He conducted a Japanese ruse by sending a small part of his fleet north to attempt to fool the US Navy. US Admiral Halsey had moved north to go after what he thought was the main Japanese fleet, but he quickly discovered the ruse the Japanese had employed and that he was following a smaller fleet. Unlike his Japanese adversary, Halsey made a leadership decision on the spot to reverse course; this move gave the US fleet the advantage in defeating the Japanese. This action would not have worked if Halsey had to get the okay from Washington. The US military leadership left the decision-making to those in the field.

Admiral Kurita was willing to accept the status-quo—the Japanese Samurai code of blind obedience—in his dire situation and resisted change, losing this critical battle, which foreshadowed the end of World War II.

Admiral Kurita went down with his ship. Admiral Halsey was not willing to accept the status-quo or the current situation, so he made the critical decision on the spot that won the day.

If this situation had been reversed and the Japanese had been willing to accept, rather than resist, a change, common sense says we may have seen a tragic outcome for US forces in this tipping point battle.

CS = PR² Lesson: Great leaders seize the moment.
They are flexible and willing to change direction to meet
any new challenges using their instincts.

11. **Know your competition as well as you know your own company.** Once upon a time, an American aircraft company and a

Japanese aircraft company decided to have a competitive crew race on Lake Washington.

Both teams practiced long and hard to reach their peak performances. The day of the big race, both teams were as ready as they could be, but the Japanese boat won by a mile.

Afterwards, the American team became very discouraged by the loss and its morale sagged. The American team's corporate management decided the reason for this demoralizing defeat had to be found as soon as possible. A continuous improvement team of executives was set up to investigate the problem and come up with a solution for appropriate action. Their conclusion was that the Japanese team had eight people rowing and one steering, whereas the American Team has one person rowing and eight people steering.

The American corporation steering committee immediately hired a consulting firm to study the management structure. After some time and millions of dollars, the consulting team concluded: Too many people were steering and not enough rowing.

So to prevent losing to the Japanese next year, the management structure had to be changed to four steering managers, three area steering managers, and one staff manager. A new performance system was implemented for the person rowing the boat to give more of an incentive to work harder and become a "Six Sigma" performer. "We must give him empowerment and enrichment," they thought. "That will do."

The next year, the Japanese won by two miles.

The American corporation laid off the rower for poor performance, canceled all capital investments for new furniture, halted the development of a new canoe, awarded high-performance awards to the consulting company, and distributed the money saved on bonuses to their senior executives.

Soon after, the Japanese company bought the American corporation and terminated all senior executives.

CS = PR² Lesson: Stop, learn, and listen. Great leaders take the time to know their competition. As Sun Tzu said, "If you know thy enemy and know thyself, you need not fear a hundred battles"

ROBERT ROSEN'S EIGHT PRINCIPLES OF LEADING PEOPLE

In his book *Leading People*, Robert A. Rosen offers eight principles for leading people. Let's briefly look at each one.

1. VISION

According to Rosen, "Leadership is the art of creating a working climate with a vision that inspires others to achieve extraordinary goals and levels of performance.

"The ultimate challenge of any leader is to create a world class organization that is both highly productive and able to withstand a competitive assault."

CS = PR² Lesson: Vision equals high performance and results.

2. TRUST

"If you don't trust your associates to know what is going on, they'll know you don't really consider them partners"

— Don Soderquist, Vice Chairman of Wal-Mart

Upward communications only take place when leaders are trusting—and trustworthy.

Leaders who create trust are:

- **Genuine:** It's important for people to touch and feel them as real people.

- **Believable:** Their word, whether spoken or written, is credible.
- **Dependable:** They make good their promises, whether declared or implied.
- **Predictable:** Being consistent makes it safe to be vulnerable and work together.
- **Benevolent:** They have the capacity to put aside self-interest for the good of the group.

CS = PR² Lesson: Trust is the glue that holds teams together.

3. PARTICIPATION

Two minds are better than one. Many minds are best. Collective wisdom is simply greater than individual insight. Leaders can tap into this collective wisdom by nurturing a team environment.

To be successful, the leaders must understand their power lies outside themselves.

If you are a good leader, when your work is done, your aim fulfilled, people will say, "We did it ourselves."

With today's associates wanting more than money and tangible rewards, leaders need to use persuasive tactics beyond the traditional carrot-and-stick approach. Understanding the nuances of various positions and building rapport with various workers allows you to take the most effective path to success without damaging relationships.

CS = PR² Lesson: We are all gifted with two ears and one mouth. Listening is the art of good leadership.

4. LEARNING

Do you accept the status quo? Are you a curious person eager to learn from others?

Are you nurturing your own personal development?
Are you being mentored or are you mentoring others?
Do you know your strengths and shortcomings?
Are you tapping into people's discretionary efforts?
Is your company a learning organization?

5. DIVERSITY

We are all different. There was a time when we checked those differences at the door, but those days are gone. Today, valuing differences is critical to business success.

The best leaders have a deep appreciation for what makes people unique.

Successful leaders understand the roots of their prejudices and are aware of their personal blind spots.

CS = PR² Lesson: Good leaders are color blind and
look to the inner souls of their associates.

6. CREATIVITY

Creative leaders see opportunities that others don't see. They entertain off-beat ideas and reconfigures problems to find new solutions.

They have faith in others' capacity and believes their organizations can solve their own problems and create new business by unleashing creativity in the workplace.

Maximum productivity comes from building on your associates' strengths and having them manage around their weaknesses.

CS = PR² Lessons: No idea is a bad idea. It is only bad when
creative, outside-the-box thinking is stifled.

Creative leaders also hire people who are flexible and inquisitive. They encourage spontaneity, nonconformity, and independent thinking

The key to innovation is good leadership. To build creative organizations, leaders must believe they have rich pools of hidden talent within their organizations.

CS = PR² Lesson: Curiosity may have killed the cat; however, the curious person will create the next earth-shattering idea.

7. INTEGRITY

Every successful leader has a moral compass—a gut sense of what is right and wrong. The best leaders walk their talk.

CS = PR² Lesson: Walk your talk!

8. COMMUNITY

It takes a mature leader to build a community. Leaders who are mature build the largest commitments and inspire the highest performance within their organizations.

Mature leaders start with a sense of purpose—a deep sense of convictions about life—that help them see what's important about business.

CS = PR² Lesson: Like a rowing team, all must pull together to win the day.

DREA'S TEN ELEMENTS OF GREAT LEADERSHIP
LEADERSHIP IS SPELLED:

L = Listen
Listen to your internal and external customers.

In the world of business/hospitality, your customers are:

Internal: Your superiors, board of directors, stockholders, and team.

External: Your buyers, guests, suppliers.

In the world of academia, your customers are:

Internal: the institution's senate/faculty, your team.

External: students, alumni, legislature

In the world of association management, your customers are:

Internal: board of directors, your team.

External: member stakeholders, suppliers (commercial and hospitality/destinations)

E = Execute

If your instincts say, "Do it now!" do it, but be accountable for your actions. Don't blame others for your failure. It is better to ask for forgiveness than to apologize for failure. Do it, and do it now.

A = Take Action

If you have a problem, take action. It won't go away so address the issue head on. Procrastination is the mother of failure, so do it now.

D = Embrace Diversity

Be willing to accept new ideas and cultures into your organization. Be open-minded to all recommendations and suggestions from every corner.

E = Make the Effort

Work hard to get good. Then work hard to get better. Learn from your mistakes.

"The level path is easy, but it will not bring you to the mountaintop."

— Dr. Idel Dream

R = Be Reasonable

Don't ask anyone to do anything you would not do yourself. Lead from in front and by example.

S = Work to Succeed

Your success will be guaranteed by working to ensure that your associates exceed beyond their wildest dreams.

H = Be Hospitable.

It is so true that you get more flies with honey than vinegar. Be gracious. Treat all with whom you work on equal terms. A smile can melt an iceberg!

I = Have Integrity.

Perhaps the most important letter in leadership is the I for integrity. Not having integrity (honesty) is tantamount to failure. No matter the cover-up, all will pay a price at some time. Remember, up can be slow, but down is very fast!

P = Be Persistent.

The sale may begin with no. Be persistent. Know your limitations, but if your heart tells you something is right to do, do it.

THE CS = PR² LEADERSHIP FOUR KS

1. Know yourself.
2. Know your internal and external customers.
3. Know your competition.
4. Know your limitations.

> *"I am a great believer in luck. The harder I work,*
> *the more of it I seem to have."*
>
> — Coleman Cox

The authoritarian Hongwu Emperor (Ming Taizu) wrote the *Six Maxims* that inspired the Sacred Edict of the Kangxi Emperor:

> Be filial to your parents
> Be respectful to your elders.
> Live in harmony with your neighbors.
> Instruct your sons and grandsons.
> Be content with your calling.
> Do no evil.

"Happiness lies in the joys of achievement and the thrill of creative effort."

— Franklin Roosevelt

CHAPTER FOUR LEADERSHIP TAKEAWAYS

- Hire the best to build your team. Build a high-performance culture. Walk your talk.
- Good leaders are not afraid to hire associates who are smarter than them.
- Listen, listen, listen, and be flexible. The best ideas come from inclusion. Listening is the art of good leadership.
- When problems arise, surprise your clients with uncommon action by acting swiftly.
- No idea is a bad idea. It is only bad when creative, outside-the-box thinking is stifled.
- Great leaders are flexible, use their instincts, and are willing to change direction to meet new challenges.
- If you believe something is right to do, have the courage of your convictions. You can ask for forgiveness later.
- Know your competition.

Some wonderful leadership quotes:

"Inspect what you expect."

— Fred Kleisner, former President of Westin Hotels

"Getting thing done through people."

— Eddie Carlson, former CEO,
Westin Hotels and United Airlines

"Trust is the most important element of any relationship."

— Milton Carney, Director of ABC meetings

"Big is not always better and never lose sight of your core competencies. We are not going to allow ever again at Starbucks for growth to cover up our mistakes. We are not going to have unbridled growth that turns into a strategy as opposed to a purpose."

— Howard Shultz, CEO of Starbucks

ROBERT ROSEN'S EIGHT PRINCIPLES OF LEADING PEOPLE

1. Vision

2. Trust

3. Participation

4. Learning

5. Diversity

6. Creativity

7. Integrity

8. Community

THE CS = PR² LEADERSHIP FOUR KS

1. Know yourself.

2. Know your internal and external customers.

3. Know your competition.

4. Know your limitations.

What three or more lessons did you learn from this chapter?

1. _____

2. _____

3. _____

PART 3

COMMON SENSE LESSONS IN MARKETING AND SALES

5

LESSONS LEARNED IN MARKETING

"Every really new idea looks crazy, at first."
— Abraham Maslow

"Don't disturb the competition while they are making a mistake. When you do so, you only enhance their brand!"
— David R. Evans

Marketing is a strategic process. Sales is the tactical process. Marketing and Sales (Chapter 6) are as different as oil is to water, so I have decided to treat each discipline with its own chapter.

DEFINITION OF MARKETING

Wikipedia defines marketing as "the study and management of exchange relationships." The American Marketing Association defines marketing as: "An organizational function and a set of processes for creating, communicating (e-marketing, advertising, public relations, research), delivering value to customers, and managing customer relationships in ways that benefit the organization and its stakeholders."

Duane Knap, author of *The Brand Mindset*, says a product must be established as a "genuine brand" before the product can be marketed and then sold, either by the direct sales (face to face) or indirect sales (web, direct mail, etc.) Wikipedia defines a sale as "the exchange of a commodity or money as the price of a good or a service." Sales is an activity related to selling or the amount of goods or services sold in a given time period.

Marketing is used to create, keep, and satisfy the customer. With the customer as the focus of marketing's activities, marketing is one of the two premier components of business management, the other being innovation. Other services and management activities such as operations (or production), human resources, accounting, and law and legal aspects can be "bought in" or "contracted out."

While this chapter focuses on service marketing, its common sense suggestions are germane to all enterprises created to get people to buy their products.

First I would like set the CS = PR^2 record straight about the hospitality industry's perception of the director of sales and marketing. This title is commonly misunderstood by hotel operators and hotel consultants. In the hotel business, "director of sales and marketing" (DOSM) was created in the late '70s and '80s to justify promotions or higher salaries.

More often than not, the best salesperson is promoted to director of sales and marketing without consideration of their skills or training in the marketing discipline, and in most cases, with these new marketing challenges, the *hotel loses the skills of its best salesperson.*

If a hotel has the good fortune to have an associate who is a DOSM skilled and trained in the marketing function, then the person leading the sales function should have the title associate director of sales, sales director, or senior sales manager.

When a property, because of size or budget, doesn't wish to have two separate positions noting the different skills sets for sales and marketing, as defined below, the ideal situation for maximum performance should be director of sales.

The director of marketing or marketing manager should report to the hotel's general manager (GM), who is in reality the chief marketing officer (CMO). The GM sets the tone and brand for the product or service.

The same can be said for any enterprise, corporation, or association—the person charged with leading the organization is responsible for ensuring the organization's brand is *genuine*, and the brand promise is always the benchmark for the organization's business plan's objectives, strategies, and tactics.

The director of sales in branded properties should focus on sales, whereas the corporate offices do the brand development and marketing. However, large complex hotels and resorts, given their unique locations and whether they are part of a chain or independent, may have a marketing manager or director of marketing on the team to add value to the corporate effort with a focus on the destination's unique attributes and features, advantages, and benefits (FABs).

In all cases, those leading sales and marketing teams should be schooled in revenue management and the complex distribution channels in the marketplace today.

The rise of associate luxury hotels, leading hotels, and preferred hotels were created by the development of non-branded properties, so independents could compete with the large global hotel brands. The hotel representation firms expanded the direct sale reach along with distribution and marketing services.

Academically, selling is thought of as a part of marketing; however, sales departments often form a separate grouping in a corporate structure.

The greatest misconception about service marketing, according to Harry Beckwith, author of *Selling the Invisible: A Field Guide to Marketing*, is that:

- Greatness may get you nowhere.

- At Focus Groups, don't stack the deck. Ask loaded questions.
- The more you say, the less people hear.
- Seeing the forest through the falling trees.

Selling the Invisible is about marketing, but not just about marketing. It addresses a broader definition that includes asking whether branding, customer service, and even the product itself are serving up what people want to buy. By presenting short, digestible bites of story and advice, the book makes you want to make a change in how you market.

The new marketing is more than just a way of doing; it is a way of thinking. It begins with an understanding of the distinctive characteristics of services—their invisibility and intangibility—and the unique nature of their service prospects and users—their fear, their limited time, their sometimes-logical ways of making decisions, and their most important drives and needs.

CS = PR² Lesson: Marketing is strategic. The big picture considers the marketing plan as the "Road map for success" (DREA) in brand development.

Here's a World War II example of strategic (long range) planning: After Pearl Harbor, the Allies realized it was a two-front war so they agreed to focus on getting Germany to capitulate first.

Here's a World War II example of tactics:
Until the full force of all the Allied forces could be devoted to defeating Japan, the US and Australian forces would island hop in the Pacific.

Following is a common sense marketing lesson from Andy Finn, former Westin sales associate and the current Executive Vice President of Benchmark Hotels:

Marketing is the art (and science) of giving customers what they want, not what *you* want.

I am a faith-based individual. I try my best to live a good Christian life (not always successfully). I don't think others are required to believe what I believe. Folks have their own convictions. They are entitled to worship in their own way and their own time. Perhaps our world might be a little better if we were to take the time to respect the right of people to worship in accordance with a doctrine that gives them peace and spiritual fulfillment. As long as, of course, a belief does not hurt others, it can be very interesting and insightful to understand (and respect!) others' religious beliefs.

"This is my simple religion. There is no need for temples; no need for complicated philosophy. Our own brain, own heart is our temple; the philosophy is kindness."

— Dalai Lama

For four years, I worked at a ski resort in Utah. I learned a lot about the ski business, and my family and I cherished the opportunity to live in the mountains. There is a certain mystique about their timelessness and beauty. Our owner, at the time, was a member of the Jewish faith. He and his family practiced Orthodox Judaism. I learned a lot about the religion in working with the owner and his family. Words like Shul, Bimah, and Shabbat, which I had not been familiar with, became meaningful. He decided to open a strict kosher restaurant at the resort that would be open during ski season (December–March). From a marketing perspective, the first challenge is sheer numbers. The number of practitioners of the Jewish faith in the US is (approximately) 5.3 million. Thirteen percent are orthodox. The number of orthodox Jews who are skiers drops precipitously. This is not to say that the restaurant was not usable by those who prescribe to the reformed and conservative movements; however, the target was clearly orthodox.

Three concerns exist in operating such a restaurant:

1. Food cost in a restaurant operation is (along with labor) the primary expense. The cost of food in a kosher establishment is astronomical. Twice as much as a normal operation in some cases. The number of certified purveyors is quite limited, and the food must be handled and processed very cautiously so as not to violate kosher law.

2. A rabbi must be present to supervise daily food purchase and preparation, as well as conduct services for the Sabbath. The rabbi and his family require living quarters.

3. An ordinary culinary expert (chef) does not suffice in a kosher establishment. The chef must have expertise in kosher food preparation.

As a result, four common sense tenets made it clear the restaurant could not be successful:

1. The audience was not large enough to match and/or justify the expenditure which, with customized equipment, was north of $1.5 million for an eighty-seat seasonal establishment.

2. Food cost is king. To price your establishment in sync with the market, you must have volume. Some hotel restaurants can rely on a robust local market to offset the times when volume, from hotel guests, drops. In the case of a kosher specialty restaurant in the mountains of Utah catering to a minute audience, the local market was non-existent.

3. In a food and beverage operation that already operates with razor-thin margins, be very careful of incurring extraneous expenses (like living expenses for a rabbi) that can obliterate the bottom line.

4. Give the customer what they want, not what you want. Understand your promise to your customer (branding), and know who you are and what your product stands for in the mind of the guest. Never deviate. Never give the customer reason to think you are something you are not.

While I admired the fact that our owner was remaining true to his faith and family, it appeared, from a business perspective, to be a questionable strategy. It seemed impossible for him to make any kind of demonstrable profit.

CS = PR² Lesson:
Give your customers what they want, not what you want!

Now for a common sense marketing lesson from Peter Smith, former Westin Vice President of the Hotel Toronto:

In 1982, Hotel Toronto had just gone through a corporate name change to the Westin Hotel Toronto and there was confusion in the market.

We needed a simple solution with big impact! We negotiated a deal with Wayne Gretzky`s agent for the use of his name in print advertising for a year. We had ads in the *Globe, Mail,* and *Toronto Sun* newspapers, and "superboards" at some of Canada's major airports with a rendering of the hotel and the caption, "Stay at Wayne Gretzky's place, The Westin Hotel, Toronto."

The ad won a national award, and people thought Wayne had bought the hotel! Weekend and corporate business went up. We did the same thing in Quebec with Guy LaFleur using the *Montreal Gazette.*

CS = PR² Lesson: More often than not, celebrities love hotels and great service. Celebrity name and face recognition can be very helpful when creating a brand, and it helps their brand.

As Duane Knapp of Brand Strategy, Inc. knows, the fundamental strategy of marketing is to create a distinctive brand! No brand, no product, no sale!

Let me share with you now a little history of the Westin/Western International Hotels chain and how it successfully marketed itself over the years.

In 1930, two hotel owners, Severt W. Thurston of Seattle and Harold Maltby of Yakima, Washington met unexpectedly during breakfast at a diner in Yakima, Washington. The competing hotel owners decided to form a management company to handle all their properties and help deal with the crippling effects of the ongoing Great Depression. The men invited Peter and Adolph Schmidt (founder and owner of Olympia Beer), who operated five hotels in the Puget Sound area, to join them. Together, they established Western Hotels. The chain consisted of seventeen properties, all in Washington except one in Boise, Idaho. This deal also created the first ever hotel reservations system.

Western Hotels expanded to Vancouver, British Columbia, and Portland, Oregon, in 1931, and by 1941, into Alaska and California, assuming management of the Sir Francisco Drake in San Francisco, the day after Pearl Harbor was bombed. By the early 1950s, Western Hotels also had properties in Montana and Utah.

Early management developed each new property individually. After more than two decades of rapid growth, many of its properties were merged into a single corporate structure in 1958, focusing on bringing the hotels together under a common chain identity. Also in 1958, Western Hotels assumed management of three hotels in Guatemala, its first properties outside the US and Canada. Western opened its first hotel in Mexico in 1961. That same year, it opened the first hotel to be both constructed and owned by the chain, The Bayshore Inn, Vancouver, BC.

The company was renamed "Western International Hotels" (WIH) in 1963, to reflect its growth outside the US. That same year, the company went public.

From November 1, 1965 to 1970, Western International Hotels had an agreement with Hotel Corporation of America (today known as Sonesta), under which all seventy-two hotels in the two chains were jointly marketed as *HCA and Western Hotels*.

From 1968-1973, Western International had a similar joint marketing agreement with UK-based Trust House Hotels.

In 1970, Western International was acquired by UAL Corporation, with Edward Carlson becoming president and CEO of UAL, Inc. and United Airlines.

Western International bought New York's iconic Plaza Hotel in 1975 for $25 million.

Western International Hotels (WIH) president Edward Carlson is credited with bringing the Century 21 Exposition to Seattle in 1962. Carlson's own napkin sketch of a tower with a revolving restaurant on top, inspired by his visit to the Stuttgart TV Tower, was the origin of the Space Needle. The chain managed the restaurant atop the Space Needle from its opening until 1982. Western Hotels also managed a floating hotel aboard the ocean liner QSMV *Dominion Monarch*, docked in Seattle harbor during the fair.

At the end of its fiftieth anniversary on January 5, 1981, the company changed its name to Westin Hotels (a contraction of the words Western International).

In 1987, UAL Chairman Richard Ferris announced a plan to make UAL into Allegis, a travel conglomerate based around United Airlines, Hertz Rent a Car, Hilton Hotels, and Westin and linked by Apollo. This strategy failed, however, and Westin was sold in 1988 to Aoki Corporation of Japan.

Westin was the first hotel chain to introduce guest credit cards (1946), twenty-four-hour room service (1969), and personal voice-mail in each room (1991).

In the 1970s, two new upstart brands came on the scene: Marriott and Hyatt. Hilton was a very well-known brand, but it did not compete with WIH in the corporate travel market, the mainstay market segment of WIH. These new hotels, unlike WIH, were named after the brand, Hyatt Hotel and Marriott Hotels, thereby creating a distinctive brand for all their properties. WIH had icon hotels listed as Western International Hotels with no brand name associated with the property, for example the St. Francis and the Sir Francis Drake in San Francisco, the Olympic Hotel in Seattle, the Hotel Georgia in Vancouver, BC, the Bayshore in Vancouver, BC, the Plaza in New York, and the Century Plaza in Los Angeles. We spent our limited advertising marketing budget to try to connect the dots between the individual hotels with our advertising and public relations initiatives.

Shortly after the name change to Westin, our Director of Advertising Ron Larue and the advertising agency of Cole and Weber came up with a campaign to connect the WIH dots with these marvelous icon hotels. They created a celebrity campaign that focused on our people with the "People make the difference campaign." While our competition was focused on their hotels and destinations, we focused on people, internal and external.

This was effective for a while, but as Hyatt and Marriott gained momentum and began to get market share, because of name and brand recognition, we had to do something to connect the dots for Westin to become a distinctive brand.

The agency had created a "double truck ad" (an ad with two facing pages) that was placed in key travel magazines and selected publications designed to attract the upscale traveler. It was a good piece, but it did not move the Westin brand meter. Our nemesis brands, Hyatt and Marriott, were winning the brand awareness day.

In the late 1980s, our senior marketing leadership took a dramatic shift. Our senior vice president of marketing was terminated and I assumed the role as interim marketing leader, reporting to the current Westin President, Dwight Call. Dwight had been named president in 1985.

I had been frustrated with our advertising messages for many years, and felt we were being substantially overcharged by our advertising agency. However, in my role as VP of Global Sales, I could do nothing to change our message or agency. What was most frustrating for me was that I was the only graduate with a communications (advertising, PR, and TV production) degree (from the University of Washington) in the entire marketing division.

So now, I had the chance to remedy the situation.

Shortly after my appointment, I called Ron into my office, advised him to contact Cole and Weber, our current advertising agency, and explain my displeasure with the fees being charged. I told him I was not a happy camper with his oversight of the agency. He was stunned, but to his credit, he took the criticism and advised the agency of my concerns.

The president of this Seattle-based advertising agency, Cole and Weber, which had represented Western International Hotels (WIH) for more than twenty-five years, *did not call me or Ron to respond to these concerns*. Instead, he called retired Gordon Bass, former President of Western International Hotels (WIH), a longtime friend of the agency's ownership and management team. Gordon contacted my boss, Dwight, the current President of WIH, who asked me to see him, and to explain what was up.

My meeting with Dwight was very cordial. I brought him up to speed regarding my concerns with the agency's fee structure. Dwight told me he'd had a call from Gordon Bass and a call from the agency's owner, who was very upset with the call from Ron Larue regarding the fee structure. The owner had reminded him of our long relationship with the agency so I should reconsider my very dramatic actions. I listened and then asked if I could gather some information to share with him. He said fine.

I contacted Ron immediately and asked him to put together the history of fees paid to the agency over the past ten years and what I recommended the standard fee should be.

I went back to meet with Dwight the next day. When I presented the data, he was stunned. He advised me to proceed and we cancelled our relationship with Cole and Weber. The agency's vice president who had the Westin account never talked to me again.

I advised Ron to find a new advertising agency, and he did—Grey Advertising in Los Angeles. Now we needed to do something clever to get the Westin Brand connected with our iconic individual properties. We needed to connect the dots.

At this time United Airlines (UAL), our parent company, was installing TVs into their cabins for movies paid for by advertisers.

I mentioned this to Ron, thinking that with our UAL ownership we might get a deal. To his credit, he presented my suggestion to our new agency and it came through with flying colors. Ron went to Los Angeles to visit the agency and was very excited with what he saw. He called me and said, "Dave, get on a plane ASAP. You will be thrilled with what you see!"

So, without delay, I was off to Los Angeles.

To say I was thrilled with what I saw is putting it mildly. The Grey Advertising team, with some Hollywood panache, had taken our Double Truck ad and put it into film. The opening scene spun like a top and then stopped to show all the properties. One by one, the individual hotels quickly settled into the centerfold.

Then reality set in. Even with special consideration from UAL, the price tag to get this done and on the airline was a whopping $600,000! It's a paltry sum by today's standards, but back then, it would have been a huge hit on our marketing budget. We had never spent this kind of money on any marketing program to date.

I told Ron to keep this under wraps because I had told no one of our plan.

So, throwing caution to the wind, I went to see Dwight and presented him with the idea. I was stunned when he asked me, "What do you think, Dave?" I paused and said, "This will be an all-time first." Dwight replied, "If you think it's the right thing to do, do it!"

Since that incredible, thinking-outside-the-box day, I have told many people how much I respected Dwight for putting his faith in my judgment. It was a perfect example of outstanding leadership and teamwork!

The video was designed to distract passengers from their newspapers or whatever they were reading and roll out all the wonderful Westin Hotels worldwide. It was indeed a very successful distraction. I used to sit next to passengers and watch with glee as they looked up, watched the video, and then took out United Airlines' *Mainliner Magazine* and started to check off the hotels they were familiar with and the hotels where they had stayed.

Then I would lean over and ask, "How many have you stayed at?"

To my very pleasant surprise, the individual hotels on the centerfold were very popular and well received. We had, at last, connected the dots. The individual Westin Hotels became an integral part of what was to become a dominant brand. Soon, the Westin Brand became a household name. It was a very distinctive brand for the individual and leisure traveler, and highly regarded as a dominant brand in the convention and group meeting market.

Of course, much of the success of this branding story is due to the superb Westin global sales office team and their leadership, namely:

SFO: Paula Crowder

LA: Sherman Elliott

Chicago: Ted Nordahl and Bob Dauner

New York: Tom Hurley and Clyde Harris

DC: Roger Smith, Tony Schopp, and Bob Bushman

London: Michael Andrea, Michael Holehouse, and Valerie Le Moignan

Paris: Ann Francois Blotin

Tokyo: Akio Hirao

Frankfurt: Andre Schober

Author and branding guru Duane Knapp, as mentioned previously, advises successful brands worldwide on the science of building genuine brands.

The major proponent of successful marketing is to create a dominant brand! Attempting to market a product that doesn't have a distinctive brand or brand strategy is no different than attempting to sell an empty suit. The question Knapp asks is, "Are you a one-of-a-kind, distinctive, genuine brand?"

Without a brand or branding strategy, any marketing efforts are a costly waste of time.

At the crux of Knapp's work is the application of common sense for his clients.

His six Common Sense Brand Rules are:

1. Always make customers feel *appreciated* and *cared* about when they have a *problem* or need help, not just when they make a purchase.

2. Make your organization's number one goal be to have the *happiest customers*, not to be the biggest or fastest growing.

3. When an organization begins to anticipate a merger, acquisition, consolidation, downsizing, or other type of corporate transaction, *focus on keeping customers happy first* and the necessary business details second.

4. *Measure, recognize, and reward* your associates who delight your customers. Focus on how your associates can keep their customers "Happy Campers."

5. Make your customers feel gratified and happy whenever the associate just answers the phone, or does their daily job.

6. Develop and commit to a customer *Bill of Rights* and make it fundamental to your organization's culture and not just policy.

So often when brands decide to make a change in their transaction process or implement a procedure that affects customers, the customer is left out of the equation.

For instance, when a retailer restricts its return policy, it can dramatically affect how its customers feel about the brand. Instead of figuring out how to make the customers feel positive about the change, most retailers simply suffer the results.

Common sense dictates that any change that will affect the customer's experience should be well thought out and implemented in a manner that makes the customer feel as good as possible.

A common sense example would be Costco. When it changed its return policy for electronics from unlimited to ninety days, it also offered a two-year extended warranty to provide peace of mind to its customers.

I encourage the reader to read Duane Knapps's excellent work on branding.

THE KEY ELEMENTS OF MARKETING

Marketing has two key elements: advertising and public relations. For the remainder of this chapter, we will focus on those two elements.

ADVERTISING

Advertising can be summed up as follows: Find out what your clients want and trigger them to buy your product or service.

In the past ten years, the marketing silo toolkit has been dramatically altered by technology and the social media revolution through such sites as Google, Bing, Facebook, and Twitter.

Print advertising is a viable marketing tool, but while once the cornerstone of any marketing campaign, now it is just another tool in the marketing tool kit. TV advertising is out of reach for most hotels and hotel groups. Because Facebook, Google, and Twitter have dramatically changed the landscape, businesses today either need to hire a social media company, consultant, or full-time associate whose purpose is to promote the company in today's complex messaging marketplace.

However, common sense is still important in this process, as noted by George Caldwell, former Westin Sales associate, who recommends that you:

- Understand the capabilities of your own hotel or business and where it might be improved to help capture a larger market share.
- Know the local market: Cover every single office building, mall, etc. within a two-mile radius of the property and larger accounts in the greater metropolitan area in which the property was located. Use the old adage "The degree of a hotel's success is directly related to its degree of acceptance in its local community."
- Create an effective advertising and PR campaign. Rarely did hotels and resorts I competed with pay much attention to the media, electronic or print. I, however, always targeted the top newspaper and magazine columnists, best radio and TV talk show hosts in both my local market and key geographic markets. I wined and dined them and made sure they were our friends and talked about us at every opportunity.

According to Hotel Online in an April 2013 article "Millennial Trends," what is changing the marketing landscape is the next generation of leaders and managers: The Millennials, those born between 1980 and 1999, who are replacing the Baby Boomers. Millennials number 79 million. Labeled as the NOW generation, they want instant gratification. This generation is tech-savvy, dominating the marketing landscape and, therefore, changing the marketing toolkit.

This generation has grown up with technology, allowing it to access information instantly while its parents and grandparents grew up with printed material and TV as their sources of information.

In the last ten years, hoteliers have come to realize the importance of social media and hiring a social media expert or retaining consultancy services in social media. Sales team associates, and meeting planners communicate almost 100 percent via email and social media. Millennials expect real-time reporting, so they feel they are in the thick of things even when they are sitting comfortably at home.

Because Millennials grew up bombarded with advertising, they are too sophisticated to be tricked by marketers. They are also not above expressing their opinions online. Sites such as Trip Advisor and Yelp are beneficial to hoteliers because they provide options to respond to negative (or positive) comments.

The blog has also changed the marketing landscape. During a website development seminar, the speaker made an excellent point regarding Facebook and blogging.

> Facebook is like planting trees in another man's yard, whereas blogging is planting seeds in your own yard, and when you plant seeds in your own yard, you increase your presence on the worldwide web and increase your search engine optimization (SEO).

Blogging is one of the most important common sense tools to have in your marketing toolkit. Millennials love blogs.

Another article from Hotel Online in April 2013, titles "Social Creatures Online and Offline" had this to say about Millennials.

> "Millennials" are social creatures online and offline. Although previous generations express trepidation that this generation will be unable to dialogue and interact with others due to their reliance on texting and other forms of communication, Millennials do, in fact, connect with their peers in ways older generations are unfamiliar with such as texting, "Facebook" message, "Gchatting," "WhatsApp," etc. The use of social media to bond with others also feeds into the "fear of missing out" where

Millennials feel the need to share their current locations, activities, and opinions with others, and this becomes their method of interaction.

This interaction includes being able to post and to "Like" or comment on a Facebook post. Such postings allow Millennials to have a much broader reach than previous generations. While members of previous age brackets may inform a few friends via phone calls about a great hotel stay, Millennials will post a picture or review that can easily reach thousands of people at once. This reach emphasizes the power and importance of receiving positive reviews or responding quickly and well to uncomplimentary comments.

A high impact social media plan increases engagement with travelers and leads to strengthened relationships, which leads to increased consideration when it comes to buy. Today, it is as important to have a strategic social media marketing plan in your marketing toolkit as it is to have loyalty program.

However, without a dominant brand or brand strategy, even the power of social media will be ineffective, so work on your brand first and foremost.

CS = PR² Lesson: When you have a branding challenge,
"build a better mousetrap" with your marketing tools.

PUBLIC RELATIONS (PR)

The dictionary defines public relations as: "The effort to maintain a favorable public image by a company, organization, or famous person."

Public relations firms and organizations are very effective at keeping brands in the public's eye and them out of harm's way when an issue might come up that could tarnish a brand. PR firms can be very effective with a new product or identifying a social issue that a brand needs help with.

PR is also about creating positive "noise" through creative activities that are outside the box and will get the attention of the news media and the public at large.

PR is often confused with promotions (an important part of the PR toolkit). Promotion is the creative use of "Op Ed" journalism and meaningful stories about your product or brand. With properties that may have limited budgets, one can, with a very creative PR agency or staff member, can get the same amount of "ink" as one might otherwise get with a very costly PR firm.

At Westin, we were very creative with our limited PR dollars. For example, part of my sales and marketing portfolio for Westin included the three "Portman" behemoths under construction at the same time in Atlanta, Detroit, and Los Angeles. John Portman was a world-renowned architect, known for his unique open atrium hotels. Creating a brand image for the Los Angeles Bonaventure Hotel in downtown Los Angeles was a challenge at best. Leading the charge was Director of Marketing and Sales Steve Gold, who had worked with me at the Century Plaza as a stellar national sales manager. The Bonaventure Hotel was a complex and very puzzling one. For that matter, all three of these new Portman-designed hotels were challenging from both an operations and marketing perspective.

Steve Gold and I were meeting with our advertising agency early on when he suggested we dissect this monster, look inside it much like an old "Queen Mary/Elizabeth" in terms of promotional schematics, and prepare a cartoon-like schematic.

We did this, added another dimension, and created a puzzle that was used as a promo piece. This promo was so successful that Westin received the Public Relations Society of America award that year for the "Most Innovative Public Relations Campaign in the Country."

In the late '80s, in addition to my Westin Sales VP responsibilities and oversight of our global sales network, I assumed responsibility for the Prince Hotels of Japan to manage Westin's Representation Agreement for its North American marketing and distribution.

These hotels were owned by Japanese multi-millionaire Yoshiaki Tsume. His brother owned the famous Seibo department store chain. This was a long dormant Westin Representation Agreement that included the Takanawa Prince and Tokyo Prince Hotels.

This relationship was started in the late '60s by CEO Eddie Carlson to expand WIH into Asia, a very visionary move.

The Prince leadership decided to build a new hotel in the Akasaka district and needed expertise in the North American market to attract the American and Canadian business traveler to this new hotel.

My Japan team included Akio Hirao, who was overseeing our Japanese sales effort, as part of WIH's global sales initiative. Akio reported to me at the time. He was the leader in Japan among his peers in the global regional office network. The team also included Jim McFarland, who was handing the Westin advertising account. In my judgment, McFarland was a creative marketing genius.

The new Akasaka Prince Hotel had a very unique architecture and an imposing presence among Tokyo hotels, so we decided to take a page from the Los Angeles Bonaventure Hotel and create a puzzle that was distributed to 6,000 travel agents in the US and Canada. When we put this puzzle in the hotel's gift shop after opening, it sold out, thereby paying for the cost of the whole promotion.

And, as previously mentioned, our creative genius, Jim McFarland, after checking all the hotel ads in Tokyo, all looking alike with pretty geishas and a Teahouse-of-the-August-Moon look, came up with a "How to Do Japan Kit" for the North American business traveler. The reader should note that at this time, many experts were trying to teach Americans and Canadians not to "step in it" while attempting to do business in Japan.

These two examples of out-of-the-box public relations and supporting advertising exceeded our expectations. In the first year, the Akasaka Prince Hotel, the new kid on the block, became fourth in awareness with our target North American markets and competitive set after Tokyo's landmark hotels Okura, New Otani, and the

100-year old, iconic Imperial Hotel located across from the Imperial Palace, home to the emperor.

My most gratifying public relations move happened in the early '90s.

In the hotel business, hosting conventions/meetings, commonly called the group market (consisting of reserving blocks of ten rooms or more), is very competitive. Hotel companies spend big bucks attempting to turn clients into friends and booking this very lucrative business.

Trade associations, the American Society of Association Executives, (the association for all organizations that each have a meeting in their own right), and the meeting planner organizations, notably the Professional Convention Meeting Planners (PCMA), Meeting Professional International (MP) Insurance Planners Association (ICPA), Incentive Conference Planners (ICPA), and Medical Meeting Planners (MMP), are all targets for the lucrative meeting market.

At the annual conventions of these meeting organizations, both branded and independent hotel companies and their sales teams go to great expense to, often putting on lavish events that could make any president, king, or queen feel envious, to gain business.

As noted previously, Westin Hotels & Resorts (WH&R) was a relativity small brand facing much larger brands like Hilton and Marriott. Because we didn't have the big bucks for lavish events, we had to be very creative. To get to host one of these meeting planner events was a coup, but it came with a substantial expenditure. Over the years, as Vice President of Global Sales, I became very concerned that we were going over the top as an industry, with these extravagant events.

In January 1994, we had the opportunity to host 2,500 of our "closest friends" (half meeting planners and half hotel "peddlers") at PCMA's annual meeting, held at our beautiful Crown Center Hotel in Kansas City. Our owners were the Hall family, owners of

Hallmark, the greeting card company. Bill Lucas, a former WH&R Associate was the president of the large Crown Center state-of-the-art indoor shopping center with Crown Center Hotel being its cornerstone.

As the host hotel company, we had to sponsor the opening event. Given my frustration over the lavish events and our limited budget, I felt we had a golden opportunity to make a statement, but still leave the assembled with a lasting memory.

At this time, I was serving as the Chairman of the PCMA Foundation Board, so, as a supplier board member, I had to be very judicious about how far outside the box I could go.

The spring of 1993, I met with the Crown Center Hotel's general manager, Jim Mogush. I told him not to breathe a word to Bill Lucas or anyone else on what I was going to suggest.

"Jim," I told him, "I want to scale back on our January 1994 opening reception. Please find a suitable charity, and we will donate a large sum of what we save from our food and beverage costs to that charity in the name of Westin and PCMA. I will be back in June to finalize the details."

When I returned in June, Jim said he had not been able to find a charity, but he had learned offhand that the Hallmark Children's Hospital, also part of Crown Center, was short on preemie baby respirators.

A light went on. This was perfect! Better yet, the hospital's key benefactor was Mrs. Hall owner of Hallmark and Crown Center.

When I asked Jim how much one baby respirator was, he came back to me with $25,000—a goodly sum in those days. Without batting an eye, I told Jim to buy one. (As Westin VP, I had approval authority for $35,000) and to "tell no one or you'll be managing an igloo on Baffin Island, Canada."

I told no one at Westin of my plan.

Jim was very diligent and kept the secret. I arrived the Friday before the 1994 annual PCMA convention, due to start that Sunday.

We had a PCMA board meeting on Saturday. I told the board at that time what we were going to do—they were stunned.

And I told Jim to advise Bill Lucas who told Mrs. Hall of our plans. Bill came back and told us that Mrs. Hall cried when she heard the news. She was on board with this plan 100 percent and was very grateful to Westin for the very generous gift.

So, on the opening night, our food and beverage display was woefully missing in grandeur and fine food. We had some basic hors d'oeuvres in the center of the ballroom. On the stage was the new preemie respirator, proudly displayed. Each attendee that night had a nametag with the picture of a new baby being saved by the new machine. Initially, the attendees were shocked by the proletarian display of food and drink.

At this time, because of my hotel NFL ties, I had a good relationship with the Hunt family, the owners of the Kansas City Chiefs, and the team's president, Jack Stedman. I called Jack to ask if the Chiefs' star quarterback could be available to make the presentation at the opening reception. The quarterback agreed, but unfortunately, he was ill and couldn't be there that night. Instead, he sent the team's star linebacker.

Thirty minutes after the reception started, I introduced GM Jim Mogush, who introduced the Kansas City Chiefs' player, who presented the preemie respirator to two hospital representatives with a note of appreciation from Mrs. Hall.

The typically loud chatting at these hotel events quickly became less than a murmur as the machine was presented.

At this moment, the world of hosting lavish event became a wonderful philanthropic event for the industry. My very worthy competitors came forward with glowing congratulations and led the crowd in a standing ovation.

The result was *Time* magazine and every industry newspaper, including *The New York Times*, wrote about the evening. The publicity for this first-ever, industry philanthropic event equated to hundreds of thousands of dollars in free advertising, far beyond anything I had envisioned. My goal had only been to do good deed and change how we did business in attracting groups.

The next year, we were in Orlando at Westin's Swan Dolphin Hotel in Disney World in partnership with the Orlando Convention and Visitors Bureau. President Bill Peepers and I gave away a heart machine for babies born with heart failure.

At the final banquet when I presented the machine to the hospital's doctors, you could have heard a pin drop. This was indeed unique given that the assembled hoteliers and meeting planners had enjoyed two hours of adult beverages with unlimited goodies.

Later, when I was going up the escalator to present this machine at the dinner following this lengthy reception, I noted that the machine was missing from the lobby where it had been displayed.

When I asked a doctor where the machine had gone, he said, "At this time, it is saving a baby." There was not a dry eye among the 3,000 people attending.

Again, we made the headlines; however, our real mission was to put our promotional dollars to a much better use than food and booze. We had been successful beyond our wildest dreams.

I share these stories and examples because Public Relations is all about the value of being creative and daring to put your career on the line for something you believe in and that will benefit your company and society in general.

CS = PR² Lesson: When you have a branding challenge, build a better mousetrap with your marketing tools.

Without a brand or brand strategy, any marketing efforts are a costly waste of time. Attempting to market a product that doesn't have a distinctive brand or brand strategy is, as Duane Knapp says, no different than attempting to sell an empty suit.

In summary, marketing" is about branding, advertising, social media, and public relations.

"The business is the brand."

— Duane Knapp

Here are some strategic and tactical common sense questions from Duane Knapp to ask yourself about hotel and destination branding:

- How good do you want to be?
- How good do you want the guest/visitor to feel?
- Are you a one of a kind product?
- Are you sure you are one of a kind?
- Do you provide or want to provide an experience that enhances one's life?
- Who are we?
- What are we?
- What do we want to be?

CS = PR² Lesson: Prepare a list of distinctive attributes that set your product apart from those of competitors.

Also, remember to ask yourself:

- How can we create a paradigm shift?
- How can we be more successful?
- Are we exceeding expectations?

CS = PR² Lesson: Public Relations/Marketing is establishing your dominant brand and your strategic "Road Map for Success."

The following are examples of very distinctive brands. They are distinctive because of effective brand development and marketing, because they provide what the customer wants, and because they are very consistent products so the customer knows what to expect.

- Coca-Cola
- Starbucks
- Campbell's
- Budweiser
- Hallmark
- Boeing
- Amazon
- Apple
- Microsoft
- Costco
- Hilton
- Marriott
- Nordstrom
- Boeing

CS = PR² LESSONS FOR YOUR MARKETING PLAN—"THE ROAD MAP FOR SUCCESS"

Marketing plans are often overloaded with verbiage. Instead, the action steps are the critical part of the plan. I learned this during my advisory years working with Vulcan, the owner and asset manager for the new Pan Pacific Hotel's development and operation.

Vulcan, owned at the time by Paul Allen, cofounder of Microsoft, is a vast real-estate company that has in its portfolio the largest privately-owned development in the country: South Lake Union in Seattle.

The new "Pan Pacific Hotel" was to be the cornerstone of this vast renewal of the northern part of Seattle nestled on Lake Union. This lake is the connection between Lake Washington and Puget Sound.

I was retained by Pan Pacific Hotels' Senior Vice President Steve Halliday, along with pre-opening interim General Manager Lloyd Daser, to serve as an advisor for all pre- and post-opening marketing and sales activities. I was to prepare a marketing plan for the new hotel. Unlike at Westin Hotels and Resorts, where we prepared pre-opening marketing plans at least twenty-four months out, Pan Pacific Hotels' management company, located in Singapore, had failed to prepare a road map for success (aka a pre- and post-opening marketing plan).

In October 2006, one month before opening, as part of our monthly meeting schedule, we met with Vulcan Real Estate teammates Vice President Ada Healy and Gary Zak, Asset Manager. At this meeting, we were directed to give a marketing budget number and to have a marketing plan ready by March 2007.

Because Vulcan is a no-nonsense numbers company, I told my Pan Pacific clients, Steve and Lloyd, that we must be "long on facts and action and short on needless rhetoric," so I created the "DREA (David R. Evans and Associates) Smart Plan Road Map for Success" for hotel marketing. It was very brief on rhetoric and focused on action steps.

The DREA Smart Plan Road Map for Success is a working document that serves as a road map, work activity schedule, and performance measurement tool for owners, management, and sales and marketing associates. The metrics in the Smart plan should be included as part of the Performance Review process for the sales and marketing team.

The DREA Smart Plan is an *inclusive process.* A hotel's executive and operations teams are an integral part of the planning and preparation of the DREA Smart Plan. This dynamic document should not sit on the shelf until year-end, but be reviewed weekly by the sales team, monthly sales team, and GM, and quarterly by the asset manager and owner. Within the plan, each associate has a mini-action plan in place.

In March 2007 we gave the plan presentation to the Vulcan team in a two-hour meeting. This very successful event was capped by a comment from Gary Zak:

> I appreciate your focus on helping us evaluate the talents and skills of prospective senior staff for the hotel, but even more valuable was the insight into brand characteristics, the vision and marketing message that forms the personality of the hotel. The Smart Plan is the best I have seen in the hotel business.

Here are some common sense lessons for creating an effective marketing plan, adapted from Harry Beckwith's book *Selling the Invisible*:

- The first rule in marketing planning is always begin at zero.
- Determine who is setting your standards—your industry, your ego, or your clients.
- Survey, survey, survey, and have a third party do these surveys.

The DREA Smart Plan Road Map for Success is in the appendix of this chapter. This copyrighted product became my distinctive brand, and the benchmark I used very effectively during my DREA advisory career.

> *"Don't disturb the competition while they are making a mistake. When you do so, you only enhance their brand!"*
>
> — David R. Evans

CHAPTER FIVE TAKEAWAYS

"Every really new idea looks crazy, at first."

— Abraham Maslow

- Marketing and sales are as different as oil to water. Marketing is the strategic process. Sales is the tactical process.
- Marketing is marketing whether it is a service (hotel, restaurant) or a product (cosmetics, automobiles, insurance, or association memberships).
- Give your customers what they want, not what you want!
- Celebrity name and face recognition can be very helpful when creating a brand, and it also helps the celebrity's brand.
- When you have branding challenge, build a better mousetrap with your marketing tools.
- Without a brand or branding strategy, any marketing efforts are a costly waste of time.
- Prepare a list of distinctive attributes that set your product apart from those of your competitors.
- Public Relations/Marketing is establishing your dominant brand and your strategic "Road Map for Success."

What three lessons did you learn from this chapter?

1. _____

2. _____

3. _____

THE DREA SMART PLAN ROAD MAP FOR SUCCESS©

The DREA Smart Plan's objective is to keep the rhetoric to a minimum and focus on performance rhetoric and measured results.

This document serves as a road map, work activity schedule, and performance measurement tool for a Convention Visitors Bureau (CVB) and its associates. The metrics in the Smart Plan should be included as part of the Performance Review process.

The Marketing Plan (Preamble & Smart Plan) is a dynamic document that should not sit on the shelf until year-end but be reviewed quarterly, at minimum, by the CVB team and board of directors.

Each associate should have a mini-action plan in place to serve as his or her road map for success.

Note: All metrics presented in this sample Smart Plan not specific recommendations; they are only examples of metrics that can be implemented.

"What gets measured, gets done!"

— Fred Kleisner, President, Westin Hotels and Resorts

"The definition of luck is when planning meets opportunity." (Author unknown). A well thought out strategic, tactical, and measurable marketing plan beats out blind luck any day.

The plan need not be complicated. Most marketing plans are long on rhetoric and short on measurable metrics with actionable time frames. This is particularly endemic in the hotel industry where plans and plan formats evolved over the years from simple sales plans to more sophisticated documents. And often, these sales and marketing plans are prepared in a vacuum that includes the general manager (GM) and the director of sales, or the director of sales and marketing (DOSM).

In the plan, the directive and goals for the next year are set down from on high. For example, "Your goals for the next year will be a $10.00 increase in your average rate, your Rev Par will increase by $5.00, your Average Daily Rate (ADR) will increase by $3.00, and your occupancy by 2 percent." Such statements are usually made with little regard to whether such goals are achievable or not. I know because I've been there and done that.

So the GM and DOSM huddle to determine how best to achieve these new performance metrics without input from a wider audience. They do an internal SWOT (Strengths, Weaknesses, Opportunities, Threats) analysis that may corroborate with the expectations from either the asset manager, or in the case of a brand, the GM's bosses within the brand.

Often, a plan template is presented that is long on facts but very short on simple action steps. The goal seems to be to wow them with facts, and thereby justify their position to engage in rhetorical garbage.

Many hospitality and travel industry sales and marketing plans are hastily prepared, not based on reality, lacking focus, and just sit year after year on office shelves taking up space.

Jim McFarland, the former partner at advertising company Ogilvy and Mather and current Director of Development and

Communications at St. Vincent de Paul, summarizes below his observations on the DREA Smart Plan:

> I did the pre- and post-opening advertising for the Pan Pacific Hotel in Seattle from 2006 to 2010. And in 2015, I did the advertising for the Tulalip Casino and Resort. In both cases, I worked with David R. Evans on the DREA Smart Plan for both properties. This road map for success was accepted by Vulcan, owner of the Pan Pacific Hotel in Seattle. Gary Zak, the Vulcan asset manager, declared it, "The best I have seen in the hotel business." The Tulip Tribal Board approved the DREA Smart plan in five minutes.

Here are some key factors to remember in creating your own Smart Plan: "Road Map for Success!"

- Hotels and resorts are not and never have been very good resource planning for marketing. They have always been sales driven, and it hasn't been until rapid development in the last twenty-five years that people thought much about "real marketing."

- Many hotel people grew up in the business believing that if you open the doors and run a clean and well-located establishment, the rest will take care of itself. Wrong.

- Introducing market segmentation—for example, business and leisure travel, group business (ten rooms or more) sports teams, advertising, and public relations—changed everything. Some hotels responded, some didn't, and some did poorly.

- The response received to marketing reveals the kinds of market planners in hotels. Poor response, poor marketing planner.

- The best marketers to come out of business schools go into packaged goods marketing where real marketing is done.

- Hotels need the help of wise, experienced sales and marketing executives and marketing planners to figure out what to do because most people wouldn't know a brand position if it bit them in the nose.

The DREA Smart Plan process does three things well. (These are comments from successful DREA clients.):

1. Creates a collaborative environment for discussing, evaluating, and developing ideas for selling and marketing.

2. Creates pathways for revenue production because you can see how the plans relate to the business and can figure out how that translates to dollars.

3. The DREA templates provide the hotel or resort with a built-in management tool to help the hotel build its future.

Other Client Comments:

- "Our team has worked hard to develop an efficient and effective approach to developing, implementing, and monitoring plan performance."
- "Utilization of the Road Map to Success will help create a well-prepared DREA Smart Plan. And we believe this is a winning formula for profitable results."
- "Winners form the habit of concentrating on what they want to have happen, (as taught by the DREA Road Map to Success), and losers concentrate on what they don't want to have happen."
- "In pressure situations, winners call up past wins while losers recall losses! Both are self-fulfilling!"

On behalf of David R. Evans & Associates, we hope you enjoy our planning and development model.

Please, note the DREA Smart Plan Road Map to Success©, DREA Reverse Marketing Plan©, and DREA Preemptive Marketing Plan© examples are for information purposes only and are not to be copied or used without paying a negotiated fee for use and without the express permission of David R. Evans, CHME Managing Director, David R. Evans & Associates (DREA).

SMART PLAN CHECKLIST FOR SWOT ANALYSIS

Item	Suggested Time Frame	Start Date	Completed Date
First Stage Value Proposition: Determine who are we, what we are, and where we want to go. Conduct SWOT Analysis.	6 hours		
Second Stage SWOT Analysis: Order or magnitude metrics Competitive Set Analysis "	6 hours		

SMART PLAN CHECKLIST FOR SITUATION ANALYSIS

Item	Suggested Time	Date Started	Date Completed
• Economic Conditions, International, Regional, Local • Smith Travel Report Analysis Current Overall Hotel Statistics • Target Audience, Business Mix Group, Individual Leisure • Competitive Set (DREA Intercept Factor) • Smith Travel Research Competitive Set Analysis • Source Markets GDS US, International • CVB Critical Path (Compression)			

Item	Suggested Time	Date Started	Date Completed
• CVB Critical Path (Pre- and Post-Activity) • Local Chamber of Commerce Activity • Current Accounts Individual, Group, and Leisure (Tour and Travel "Individual and Tours") • Key Performance Objectives (Overall) • Key Performance Indicators (Overall) • Summary and overall position statement	8-16 hours		

SMART PLAN CHECKLIST FOR SALES AND CATERING

Item	Suggested Time	Date Started	Date Completed
Sales Plans by Segment Key Performance Objectives Key Performance Indicators (KPIs) SMART Plan Activity Schedule	TBD		
Catering Sales (Local) Key Performance Objective Key Performance Indicators SMART Plan Activity Schedule	TBD		

Item	Suggested Time	Date Started	Date Completed
Catering Sales (Group Meetings & Tours) Key Performance Objectives Key Performance Indicators SMART PLAN Activity Schedule	TBD		

SMART PLAN CHECKLIST FOR MARKETING SERVICES

Item	Suggested Time	Date Started	Date Completed
Website Assessment and Relevance Key Performance Objectives Key Performance Indicators	TBD		
Social Media Assessment and Relevance Key Performance Objectives Key Performance Indicators SMART PLAN Activity Schedule	TBD		
Other Key Destination Amenities Condominiums, Casino, Golf Course Marina, Theme Park Key Performance Indicators SMART Plan Activity Schedule	TBD		

SEGMENT: DIRECTOR OF SALES AND MARKETING

KEY PERFORMANCE INDICATORS

- Meet/exceed total 2012 revenue goal for resort.
- Have a Top 3 ranking for search engines and social media that is active and responsive.
- Provide website that has relevant content and up-to-date information that is top in our market.
- Create branding promise that can be communicated to all media outlets.
- Have the most effective and productive sales team in the market.

OBJECTIVES

- Use website and social media to showcase the resort's unique location and amenities.
- Keep the website relevant with virtual tours for prospective planners and transient guests.
- Enhance Alderbrook position to meeting & event planners as top Northwest location for corporate retreats and destination weddings.
- Conduct monthly sales team meetings to maximize group bookings and revenue.
- Maximize advertising budget through media trade, PR exposure, Eblasts and social media outlets. Continue to review communications, advertising, public relations, and social media to ensure that the most effective vehicle is being used to improve customer awareness.
- Provide a branding promise that will set Alderbrook Resort apart from its competition.
- Effective team communication between resort, duo PR and social media contact to ensure we all are working toward the same message and goals.
- Keep the SMART plan up to date and relevant by conducting weekly reviews (sales team), monthly reviews (sales team and GM), and quarterly reviews (team, GM, and asset manager).

SALES

Specific	Measurable	Actionable	Reasonable	Time Bound
Strategy	Target Metrics	Accountable	Tactical Steps	Due Dates
Provide sales leadership, tools, and information to assist sales team to reach quarterly goals.	Weekly/monthly on property sales meetings. Sales team goals will meet/exceed: Revenue: $1.821 million ADR: $163.35 Room Nights 11,150	INSERT SALES TEAM RESPONSIBLE INITIALS HERE	Conduct monthly meeting with sales staff to review revenue and rate strategy.	Monthly
Keep the 2012 Smart Plan relevant and up-to-date.	Review weekly with the sales PR and advertising team. Monthly add the General Manager (GM) to the review list.	Director of Marketing Director of Sales		Weekly Monthly with GM
Keep the sales team book of accounts relevant. Purge non-producing accounts and replace with new accounts.	Build on the Resorts 40% Repeat Business.	Sales Team	As an integral part of the sales meetings, review the account list.	Monthly
Maximize total resort revenue- Rooms, F&B and Spa	Achieve total hotel revenue of 9.4 million.	Sales and Marketing team	Discuss next 30/60/90-day strategies and opportunities	Bi-weekly

Sales team will attend selected industry events to continue to build awareness for the resort.	Regularly attend MPI, WSAE, CVB and South Sound. Wedding publications	Sales Team	Provide ads in relevant regional meeting publications and participate in tradeshows in greater Seattle and Portland areas.	Quarterly
Remain top of mind with Seattle Convention and Visitors Bureau	A minimum of one in-person contact at the CVB once a quarter. Conduct a minimum of 3 (STA) familiarization trips to the resort		Ensure that resort is exposed to additional customer familiarization trips from Asia planned by the CVB Seattle Tourism Authority (STA) in 2012.	Quarterly
Maintain the competitive edge over the competitive set.	Conduct one comprehensive competitive set on site review per quarter.	Sales Team	Stay up-to-date on what the competition is offering or upgrades to facilities.	Quarterly
Provide leadership to the catering sales team to ensure the resort is top of mind with the consumer.	Will meet/exceed 2012 catering revenue goal $2.4 million		Monthly meetings to stay on track with wedding and group business with catering and sales team	Monthly

MARKETING

Specific	Measurable	Actionable	Reasonable	Time Bound
Strategy	Target Metrics	Accountable	Tactical Steps	Due Dates
Be current on all social media outlets and top ranking for SEO.	Top 5 SEO Rankings Build Facebook Friends to 10,000.	MC/MM/FK	Update Facebook, Google+, Foursquare, and others. Also finalize keywords for SEO optimization.	January
Expand and build Alderbrook's database	Build targeted database to $30K	Market Research	Use database to send out targeted eblasts.	Bi-weekly
Partner with advanced media to work with targeted radio stations for campaigns to be conducted in the spring & winter.	Run targeted radio ads for spring and winter business	Director of Marketing Advertising Agency	Use $85K in radio ad buy with half of that being in trade to maximize advertising dollars.	January/ May/Oct
Run ads in regional bridal magazines to provide awareness of Alderbrook as top destination for weddings.	Run ads in *Seattle Bride, Portland Bride, Seattle Metropolitan, B&G,* and South Sound wedding publications.	Director of Marketing Advertising Agency	Advertise with regional bridal magazines with long shelf-lives and favorite tradeshows for new brides.	Seasonal

Use Living Social and other group buying sites to expand our customer base and build our database.	Offer Living Social or other web coupons in need periods.	Director of Marketing	Offer special deals through group buying sites during need periods.	Need basis
Use Trip Advisor to increase resort awareness.	Respond to all Trip Advisor comments, good and bad, within 24 hours.	Director of Marketing Advertising Agency	Review Trip Advisor daily	
Offer Alderbrook gift cards to 3rd parties to increase sales and exposure.	Meet or exceed 2012 Occupancy 67.6 % ADR $167.97	Director of Marketing		
Use Public Relations effectively to increase resort awareness.	% of overall PR impressions will increase by 15% over 2011.	Director of Marketing Public Relations (PR) team member PR service	Work with PR team to come up with creative and interesting pitches.	Bi-Weekly
Create a unique guest takeaway.	Implement a creative resort memory. e.g., replicas of Alderbrook Resort and "Yes" campaign	Director of Marketing Director of Sales	Make the resort "one of a kind."	January
Keep social media relevant. Communication with resort, PR & social media.	Update action plans.	Director of Marketing General Manager	Conduct monthly meeting to communicate upcoming events to stay current on action plans.	Monthly

Work with Talus Mobile to develop app for Alderbrook Resort through Bizmote	Create App to be ahead of the competitive set.	Director of Marketing Advertising Agency Telus Mobile	Work with Talus to find GPS hotspots that will signal guests' Smartphones throughout entire resort grounds.	February
Work with Wallop Creative to upgrade current meeting and wedding sections.	Create a virtual tour of the meeting's landing pages.	Director of Catering	Upgrading meetings and wedding sites will give sales team the ability to conduct a virtual tour of the resort.	As needed

6

LESSONS LEARNED IN SALES

"Selling is the art of closing the business and making the deal.
The sale begins with NO!"

— David R. Evans

THE DEFINITION OF SALES

Sales is an organizational function that builds relationships, *direct and indirect*, to introduce a products or services' value proposition. A successful sale is when a customer believes the proposed value proposition and purchases the product or service.

Note: A product must be established as a "genuine brand" before the product can be marketed and then sold either by the direct sales (face to face) or indirect sales (web, direct mail, etc.)

Before we get into this chapter, let's look at some of the related strategies covered in detail in the next chapter that relate to professional selling. Here they are as described by Wikipedia:

- **Marketing:** Defined as an ongoing process of planning and executing the marketing mix (Product, Price, Place,

Promotion) for products, services, or ideas to create exchange between individuals and organizations.

- **Advertising:** Defined as a form of communication that typically attempts to persuade potential customers to purchase or to consume more of a particular brand of product or service.
- **Public relations:** Defined as the practice of managing the flow of information between an organization and its audiences.
- **Sales Promotions:** Defined as the pre-determined actions designed to increase consumer demand, stimulate market demand, or improve product availability for a limited time (i.e., contests, point of purchase displays, rebates, free travel, and sales incentives).

Selling in the hospitality world, unlike product selling, didn't arrive on the hotel scene until after World War II. Prior to then, hotels filled their guest rooms with business travelers and vacationers, and for the most part, had relatively small meeting space, usually reserved for social events.

During the post-war era, many new, upgraded large hotels, with ballrooms and meeting space, sprung up all over the country. These changing times required a change in operating philosophy and adding a salesperson(s) to the hotel staff. As previously stated, hotels in New York and Chicago were the first in the industry to begin this process.

Heretofore, sales was the purview of the catering department, but the changing marketplace required that hotels create full-fledged professional sales departments for the first time since "inn keeping" started in ancient times.

Steve Halliday, the very successful general manager for the Pan Pacific Hotel in Vancouver, BC, shares a common sense statement about sales:

Nothing happens until you sell something! David R. Evans taught me that! Sales must happen first, and most importantly at the right, agreed-upon targeted price. The GM or top person must be the Chief Sales Officer and let the staff know about the importance of sales. Then they will feel it and the customers will see it. This truth is not limited to the hotel business. Every CEO must represent the company's brand, know the customer, and, as Bill Marriott said, provide "management by walking around."

Selling is an art form that requires you to be creative and always prepared to think outside the box if you want to hit the hot button of your potential customer. Remember, as David Evans says, "Sales begin with a No" so you need to be prepared to respond to that "No" to turn it into a "Yes."

CS = PR² Lesson: The sale begins with No! To close the deal, find the hot button and think outside the box.

Here is a common sense lesson on closing the deal from my own experience as a free agent signer for the Seattle Seahawks in the mid-1980s.

The Dallas Cowboys used independent free agent signers to sign free agents. Potential players became free agents when they were not drafted.

Gil Brandt, Director of Player Personnel for the Dallas Cowboys, realized many players slipped through the NFL draft for one reason or the other, so within the free agent pool were potential superstars. The Dallas Cowboys became very successful with these undrafted players. Brandt create a pool of free agent signers from ex-NFL players and successful local business types, who could sell, and had played the game of football in the past in college or in the NFL.

The free agent signers would be assigned a territory where Brandt had identified an excellent prospect. The signers' travel and expenses were paid by the Cowboys. They would then be sent out to their territories with the prospects' names in hand so when the NFL draft for the current year started, they would be in position to sign the prospective player before any other team had a chance.

This brilliant strategy built the Cowboys into Super Bowl champs and an NFL powerhouse for years.

When Dick Mannsberger, Brandt's # 2 at the Cowboys, moved to Seattle to become the Seattle Seahawks' Director of Player Personnel, he brought the same free agent signing plan to the Seattle Seahawks.

The Seahawks' independent signers would be on the road a few hours before the NFL draft closed, "camping" outside the home of the prospect, waiting for the call from the Seahawks' starter. After the draft was over, they would knock on the prospect's door and hopefully convince him to sign the standard NFL player contract, which included bonus clauses. (I should note here that all NFL players, whether millionaire superstars or free agents, signed the same NFL contract.)

Now, in some cases, to beat the competition, we would try to get the player out of his home to some obscure place for coffee, and more often than not, this was in the wee hours of the morning. This practice was used by Brandt and copied by the Seahawks. This practice caused so much contention from other teams that Commissioner Pete Rozelle create the "Brandt rule": No NFL prospect can be contacted until the draft is concluded." This rule ended the practice of late-night coffee klatches. A free agent signer could sit with the potential signee until the draft was over, but he could not take him away from his home.

It goes without saying that players who were not drafted were not happy campers. Having been college superstars, this was the first time in their lives they had been rejected. As a result, the signer had to "walk softly" to appease the prospect, who was still reeling from his rejection in the draft, and sell him on the fact that the door was not closed to NFL stardom because signing as a free agent was his second chance.

In 1982, I was sent to Los Angeles to sign a Seahawk prospect Norm Johnson, an outstanding kicker for UCLA. At the time, the

Seahawks were not happy with Efren Herrera, a great place kicker, but he could not get the ball past the 20-yard line on kickoffs.

Norm wasn't drafted, so I was assigned to sign him to the Seahawks. However, he had other suitors: the Chicago Bears and Denver Broncos.

Now for the challenge!

The Seahawks' signing bonus was $5,000, whereas the Bears and Broncos' was $10,000. The Seahawks would not budge on its signing bonus because it didn't want to set a precedent with other potential free agents. Secondly, the Broncos and Bears had a position for Norm, while the Seahawks still had Herrera on the roster.

So when I first met with Norm at UCLA's campus, I was starting with a decided disadvantage. However, the good news was that we met during the day. I didn't have to get him out of bed at midnight or later.

As an aside, during his past season at UCLA, Norm kicked the winning field goal to beat the USC Trojans. That put my alma mater, the University of Washington, in the Rose Bowl.

To break the ice, I thanked Norm for putting the Huskies in the Rose Bowl, and as token of my Husky appreciation, welcomed him to Seattle and the Seahawks.

Well, Norm had an agent, Bruce Singman, a Beverly Hill lawyer (UCLA Alumni) who was a time agent. Singman wanted the big bucks for Norm and would not budge for the lower signing bonus. We went back for forth for three days.

During those three days, I got to know Norm on a personal basis. We discussed life after football, and during these conversations, I learned he was ten credit hours short of graduating from UCLA.

Norm was now leaning toward the Broncos. His agent was becoming a real pain, with no flexibility. Even after I had pointed out that Norm would start and the wonderful features, advantages, and benefits of Seattle over Denver.

I finally got fed up with Norm's agent, Singman. No matter what we offered, he would change the ground rules, so I returned to Seattle with an unsigned Norm Johnson. Dick Mannsberger was not pleased. He said he had talked to Norm's agent, who said I was "a tough SOB," and indicated that Norm liked the Seahawks' opportunity, so he wanted to know what could be done to make the deal.

Mannsberger called me and said, "Do whatever you can to sign Norm Johnson." Seahawks Head Coach Mike Holmgren lived just down the road from me on Mercer Island, so I called Mike and asked him if I could use his home office to close the deal with Johnson. I went to his home and spent the weekend closing the deal.

That weekend, I spent more time talking to Norm about life after football than did the other signers who focused only on football. I learned that Norm wanted his college degree.

So I called our UW alumni director to see if Norm could take courses at UW so he could graduate. Yes, he could, and UCLA would accept the ten hours from UW for Norm to get his degree.

Mannsbeger told Norm's agent we were set to get Norm enrolled at UW so he could graduate. This was the point of difference in this sale.

The rest is history. Norm Johnson replaced Efren Herrera. He played for the Seahawks from 1982 to 1990 and became the first Seahawks free agent all pro. Plus, he graduated from UCLA!

I was later honored to be part of Norm's wedding. After football, he became a very successful real estate agent in the Seattle area.

When Norm was asked later in his career why he had chosen the Seahawks, he said, "Evans was the only one who cared what happened after my NFL career was finished."

CS = PR² Lesson: To close the deal, find the point of difference in the sale.

When selling, one often must be creative—and prepared to stick your neck out, with the off-chance it may get cut off.

The Anheuser-Busch (AB) annual distributor meetings were a gem, with 2,500 distributors attending them in different large market cities. In 1967, AB was planning to extend its brewing operations to Los Angles so that was a target year for this meeting.

However, the competition was not Los Angeles. Why?

There was no ballroom space large enough in Los Angeles. The AB distributors' meeting had outgrown the Beverly Hilton in San Francisco, so "nearby" Las Vegas was a very formidable competitor with its wonderful, large hotels like the Sahara and Caesar's Palace and the added lure of spectacular entertainment and gaming. Las Vegas would work well for this meeting because of its proximity to Los Angeles.

I knew that to get this incredible group's business booked at the Century Plaza would be a major sales success story, and send a message to the Las Vegas hotels, that the new "grande dame," the Century Plaza had arrived on the hotel scene.

The point person for the AB distributors' meeting was AB's Director of Distributor Relations, Keith Flower. I had first met Keith when I had made a sales call on him at the AB home office in St Louis, Missouri, when I was a pre-opening sales manager. Now when I called him, I convinced him he should come see the Century Plaza while we were in construction. Keith was very apprehensive of committing to a new hotel, especially one that didn't yet have a track record of success.

Keith, however, agreed to visit in the spring of 1965, a year before opening. I met Keith at the Los Angeles airport in our hotel limousine. At that time, I decided not to take the traditional ride up the "405 Freeway" to "Santa Monica Boulevard", but the "back" way on the "surface" street, via "Sepulveda" Boulevard" and through the upscale the "Cheviot Hills" residential area.

Why this route?

Because, on the way in Culver City, we passed the famous MGM studio backlot, going by the sound stage where *The Wizard of Oz* was filmed, on through the upscale Cheviot Hills residential area, passed the Hillcrest Golf Club (home for all the great comedians like Jack Benny) to the "20ᵗʰ Century Fox Studios." The under-construction Century Plaza was just behind Fox Studios, so it was then on down Century Boulevard to our construction site.

This brief tour of Los Angeles gave Keith a different perspective on Los Angeles. He got a sense of the Hollywood experience and our location at the center of the movie business. This was the first time we used this arrival plan for our meeting planners. Keith was duly impressed—it was a view of Los Angeles he hadn't expected, complete with no freeways. We learned an important lesson from this pickup experience—by taking this route, we dispelled the notion that Los Angeles was spread out with freeways everywhere. This became our modus operandi for the arrival of all future meeting planners and VIPs.

The Hollywood tour from LAX via Sepulveda Boulevard became one of our most valuable USPs (unique selling points). All planners and VIPs came with the standard image, portrayed by Bob Hope and other entertainers, that Los Angeles was spread out with freeways everywhere and no typical downtown. We changed this perception forever.

CS = PR² Lesson: Dare to be different when establishing USPs.

I broke the ice with this first visit, and Keith wanted to return and review specifics.

Since we were a year from opening, Keith had to be convinced that we could do the job. First, we had the largest ballroom, at 24,000 square feet, of any hotel in Las Vegas or Los Angeles. Keith anticipated we would have a least 2,400 AB distributors, families, and friends at this first-ever Los Angeles Anheuser-Busch meeting. While our new ballroom was a very distinct USP, we were an untried hotel. When Keith expressed concern, I told him we could measure up to task. "Keith, no risk, no gain." Later, I learned he had told other hoteliers he was impressed with my confidence—that was the tipping point.

Secondly, to the credit of our managing director, Harry Mullikin, we were about to set the entire North American hotel business on its ear with room service liquor at package store prices. No longer would we gouge guests with expensive room service liquor. This was another USP that really hit home with Keith.

When Keith came back a couple of months later, he noticed our new spectacular flagpole at the hotel entrance of the half-moon driveway off the Avenue of the Stars.

As we were getting close to closing the deal, Keith asked me, "Dave can we fly the Anheuser-Busch A & Eagle flag on the flagpole, so when Mr. (August) Busch arrives on Sunday to start our meeting, he will see his spectacular flag flying proudly?"

For a moment, I was lost for words. Our Century Plaza flagpole was sacrosanct. Only the Star Spangled Banner was to fly high and proudly on our Century Plaza flagpole.

I pondered the question and decided if this were a deal breaker, I would take a chance. "Keith, yes!" I exclaimed.

Soon after, following numerous phone and in-person meetings, Keith called and said, "David, we will be at the Century Plaza in January 1967." We would be hosting AB six months after we opened. The sale was made!

So at 7 a.m. on a Sunday in January, Bodo Lemke, our convention service manager, and I lowered our US flag to place the "A & Eagle" flag below it. We then raised both flags. Mr. Busch arrived in our hotel limo that afternoon and noted with glee that his company flag was flying proudly from our flagpole.

The first ever Anheuser-Busch was off to a fine start, but Bodo and I wondered what would happen Monday morning when our boss, Harry Mullikin, saw this flag on the flagpole.

Well I got my answer the next day!

I was enjoying a cup of coffee when I received a tap on my shoulder. It was Harry. I expected to get a real chewing out, but Harry just said, "David, next week are you planning to fly a scrap car off our flagpole." The next week the Institute of Scrap Iron and Steel would be meeting at the hotel. I got the message. The A & Eagle remained until the Anheuser-Busch meeting was over. After that, no other flag ever was raised on the CPH flagpole.

The good news is that the Anheuser-Busch meeting returned to the CPH every other year in January for ten years, bringing in close to $4 million in hotel revenue. Keith Flower also became my lifelong friend.

I often wonder what would have happened if I had said no, or even hesitated and said I had to check first.

CS = PR² Lesson: It is better to act on our instincts than ask for forgiveness later. A USP can close the deal.

During the third year of the AB distributors meeting at the Century Plaza, I learned a valuable sales lesson from August Busch: "Making friends is our business."

The general format for the AB meetings was arrival on Sunday, with receptions on Monday and Tuesday, meetings with lunch and dinner both days, and a trade show in the adjacent drive to the underground ballroom. All events were attended by 2,400 Anheuser-Busch distributors, executives, and their families.

At all social events, I accompanied Keith Flower. It was standard operating procedure for our sales teams to remain connected with their groups while they were at the hotel.

That year on Tuesday, I was with Keith at the luncheon. "Gussy" Busch, as he was fondly addressed, enjoyed a few martinis. Keith, jokingly muttered to me to be sure Gussy didn't fall backward off the dais. At each event, Gussy addressed the assembled group. On this day, he got up after a few martinis at lunch and asked the group:

"What business are we in?"

As the centerpiece at each table was a bottle of gin, a bottle of vodka, a bottle of bourbon, and a six-pack of Budweiser (Bud Light and Michelob were in the future), so, needless to say, all attendees were very happy campers.

One of those happy campers rose and replied in a loud Texas Drawl:

"Gussie, we'all are in the beer business."

There was pause in the room while Gussy stood for a minute and then made a response that has resonated with me forever:

"No, making friends is our business!"

Gussy sat down, and the room went silent. These few insightful words became Anheuser-Busch's brand value proposition for years, and as a result, the company had market ownership for many years to come.

CS = PR² Lesson: Turning a client into a lifelong friend
is the formula for successful selling.

In 2500 BC, Sun Tzu, the Chinese military strategist wrote:

"Know thy enemy [customer] and know thyself and one need not fear a hundred battles."

Your sales team are the frontline soldiers, the tactical unit (and marketing is the strategic unit) that will win the day, close the business, and make the deal. Of course, your customers are not your enemies—unless you disappoint them.

We often hire salespeople who have the natural gift of the gab. That is the good news; the bad news is, more often than not, while salespeople are gabbing, they are missing the more salient point of selling—getting to know the customer—and later they will wonder why they lost the business. They have failed to learn their prospects' hot buttons, or what makes them tick.

The art of selling is like a car at a railroad crossing. You must stop, look, and listen. In sales, being curious and getting to know your customer and building long-term relationships is the cornerstone of making the sale.

> *"A single conversation across the table from a wise man*
> *is worth a month's study of books."*
>
> — Chinese proverb

CS = PR² Lesson: Curiosity is the benchmark of good salesmanship.

Let me now share a common sense story about the importance of being curious, listening, and getting to know your prospect.

Shortly after the merger of Sheraton Hotels and Resorts and Westin Hotels and Resorts into the Starwood Hotels and Resorts, I was promoted to Senior Vice President of Industry and Client Relations. One of my first actions in my new position, was to visit the new Starwood Global offices. The first one I visited was the Chicago Starwood Sales Office, where I made calls with members of the sales team.

One very specific experience comes to mind.

When we called on a large association customer in Chicago, we arrived early for the meeting. It is always better to be five minutes early than one minute late. The sales associate was making small talk with me while we looked over organizations' publications in the waiting area. While he was talking, I picked one publication up and noticed some interesting information about the organization. The salesperson continued with the small talk, overlooking that I was reviewing the association's publication.

Our appointment came and went. During the meeting, the sale associate rambled on about Starwood Hotels and Resorts, never once stopping to ask a question about the prospect or the organization. When we had finished, the prospect was gracious and pleasant and thanked us for coming by.

After we left, I suggested we stop somewhere for a cup of coffee. During coffee, I asked the salesperson a couple of questions: What college did our customer attend, and did you know the organization was having a management shuffle? The response was a predictable "No"!

This salesperson had broken the cardinal rule of good selling by not taking the time to "stop, look, and listen." He came away with no "hot button intelligence" at all. I am certain our customer had mumbled under his breath, "I'm happy they're gone."

The good news is I had a long relationship with this prospect and before we called I had told him I had "set him up" to train this salesperson to do better. Now, over coffee, I proceeded to make the following common sense recommendations to my sales colleague for a successful sales call:

1. Get to the appointment early. While waiting, seek out organization publications and read them. Organizations have egos and love to share their good stuff in their publications. You'll find valuable info there.

2. Ask questions about the organization or corporation. Customers love to talk about their organizations and companies.

3. Ask "How can we best serve you?"

4. Look around at the customers' walls. This tells one a great deal about the prospect.

5. Stop, look, and listen.

6. Ask for the business!

Paul Crowder, former Westin Regional Office Sales Director, shares an excellent example of why one should not waste time fishing in an empty pond.

Regarding tradeshows and sales trips, a lack of common sense and good judgment prevail when a hotel team decides to send salespeople to cities where they don't belong!

For instance, when a regional/urban hotel's main business comes from within a 100-mile radius of their own location, sending a salesperson to a big city three or five hours away by plane to make sales calls or attend tradeshows produced by the company with global customers located in the big city is a huge waste of money and sales time. No business for them there. Even when an RSO (regional sales office) or big hotel in the big city tells the inappropriate hotel this is not the market for them, they *still* make the trip!

I have witnessed this *so* many times! Throwing good dollars after bad dollars!

The rifle shot approach to sales never works. Creating and building relationships takes time, creativity, ingenuity, and patience, just like building a structure one brick at a time.

CS = PR² Lesson: Don't waste your time fishing in an empty pond. Know thy customer: stop, look, and listen.

In my role as Vice President and General Sales Manager of Westin Hotels and Resorts and later as Senior Vice President of Industry Relations of Starwood Hotels and Resorts, I would strongly suggest to our participating sales associates that a reasonable target for them when attending planner conventions was to try to "turn *one* customer a day into a friend."

This directive's objective was to get to know the target client "upfront and personal." Sales associates' goal should be to make one new client/friend for each day at the convention; then, in time, they will have a database of "friends" rather than clients.

In my role, as the senior person overseeing these events, during the event's pre-convention meetings I advised that the sales associates must arrive at least fifteen minutes before the events started each day. These social events are when one builds relationships by *targeting the client and making initial contact.*

And, to set themselves apart from their competition, they needed to *be seen where they least likely to be seen.* This meant attending the meetings designed for the organization's attendees, not their suppliers. While the topic may be boring and irrelevant, one will most likely be the only hotel salesperson in the room, thereby having a competitive advantage. This should be common practice for all industry events attended by sales associates since the goal in attending is to maintain relationships, create new friends, and close a sale.

CS = PR² Lesson: Don't rifle shoot. Build relationships one brick at time, and do the unexpected: Be seen when you are not expected to be seen.

I learned another valuable common sense lesson early in my hotel sales career: *If all else fails, seek out the most dominant decision maker!*

In my very early days as sales manager for Western International's Olympic Hotel, Seattle's iconic hotel, I was directed by Bob Thompson, our director of sales, to venture to San Francisco and promote our new USP: the parking garage across the street.

So off I went to San Francisco where I stayed in the wonderful Saint Francis, located on Union Square. On my prospect list was Crown Zellerbach, one of the nation's leading paper companies, whose sales and management team made frequent business trips to Seattle.

I had no idea whom to call. Crown Z didn't have a sophisticated travel department, which would not become an industry standard until the 1970s. I had to be resourceful and seek out a decision maker. Logic would say that would be the CEO; however, it was unlikely he would see some salesperson without an appointment. I decided to check the reader board for the second-in-command two Crown Z executive. Then I ventured up to executive offices on the top floor without an appointment to see Crown Z's executive vice president.

I was very nervous; however, nothing ventured, nothing gained. I arrived at the executive offices, went to the executive vice president's secretary and introduced myself. She asked if I had an appointment. "No," I said and told her why I was there. She was very gracious and told me to wait in the foyer. I was now having second thoughts. About five minutes later, she came out and told me the vice president would see me now.

So I ventured into this large office, and sitting behind a very imposing desk was a very large man with a strong sense of authority. He told me to sit in the chair in front of his desk. After a minute, which seem like an eternity, he said, "Do you know why I agreed to see you without an appointment?" Stunned, I let out a very nervous "No."

He replied that he wanted to meet the young man who the gumption to call on the executive vice president of a major company without an appointment. I responded with my explanation. He then congratulated me on my creativity, entrepreneurship, and downright boldness.

He became very gracious, inquiring about my background and role at the Olympic. Then he told me he would advise all the Crown Z departments that traveled to Seattle about our new garage and hotel renovations.

The sale was made!

On a later trip to Seattle, we met again. I introduced him to our Managing Director, Tom Gildersleeve. "Mr. Crown Z" became a regular visitor to the Olympic.

I was told later by a Crown Z Olympic Hotel visitor that the executive vice president had shared my surprise visit with the CEO and Crown Z's traveling sale team. He told them my example of creative sales should be a best practice for the company.

CS = PR² Lesson: If all else fails, seek out the
most dominant decision maker.

Here's an excellent common sense lesson from George Caldwell, former Westin Hotels Director of Sales. George discusses conventional wisdom.

I find I was successful in nearly every case by following the conventional wisdom of doing the basics, which my predecessors had either not done or had not contemplated in the original planning. I always felt a successful sales and marketing plan would include the following basics:

- **Gathering good market intelligence:** This includes examining and evaluating existing market sources and feeder markets. So often we become so engrossed with our own company's goals and objectives that we overlook the competition.
- **Knowing your competition:** This requires reading their reader boards daily or hiring a service to do so. If possible get your hands on their marketing sales plan. (I would often hire the number one or two salesperson from at least two top competitors.) Ask asking the major known accounts in the marketplace what they liked about the competition and whom they liked best. Creating a reverse marketing plan on key competitors (an idea I think I got from you back in 1970). One thing I found to be true most of the time was my competitors were usually good salesmen but lousy marketers!
- **Understanding your hotel's capabilities:** This includes knowing where your hotel might be improved to help capture a larger market share.
- **Knowing the local market:** Cover every single office building, mall, etc. within a two-mile radius of the property and larger accounts in the greater metropolitan area in which the property was located. Apply the old adage: "The degree of a

hotel's success is directly related to its degree of acceptance in its local community."

- **Creating an effective advertising and PR campaign:** Rarely did hotels and resorts I competed with pay much attention to the media, either electronic or print. I always targeted the top newspaper and magazine columnists and best radio and TV talk show hosts in both my local market and key geographic markets. I wined and dined them and made sure they were our friends and talked about us at every opportunity.

Needless to say, Dave, I could go on and on about websites and social media—the newer ways to reach out that were initiated staring in the early to mid-1990s...as well as all the other aspects of marketing hotels and resorts, such as branding, image, and positioning...but I think you know all this as well as I do.

As a David R. Evans' addendum to George's wonderful remarks: Examine and evaluate existing market sources and feeder markets.

In regards to asking the major known accounts in the marketplace what they liked about the competition and which of your competitors they like best, this strategy applies to all sales, whatever the products your competitors are selling in the marketplace. The fastest downhill path to failure is arrogance and thinking your product has no peer. Even if you own the market, always be wary of that new product that may surface.

For example, I learned a very valuable lesson during my days as director of sales at the Century Plaza Hotel when our resident manager, Dan McClaskey, asked me, "How much do you know about the Marriott at the LA airport that is soon to open with over 750 rooms and a large ballroom?"

This question triggered a thought: Why not have one of my sales managers become the Los Angeles Marriott Hotel Director of Sales, in mind only, and create what I called a "Reverse Marketing Plan."

Pat Daniel, one our stellar Century Plaza Sales team members, was selected for this task. He created an excellent document that became our benchmark to compete with any "new kid (hotel) on the block.

Later, during my consulting years (2002 to 2017), I formalized my Reverse Marketing Plan format to create simple competitive set analysis for developer's market studies, which came to be named "Preemptive Market Studies." A sample of the "DREA Reverse Marketing Plan" is in this chapter's appendix.

No matter what activity the associate is involved with, a prompt follow-up is a must. Often after the heat of battle and the aura of a fast-paced industry trade show, the shoe is dropped when the associate gets back to the office and is distracted by on-site duties.

> *"It took me one day to write seven pages,*
> *but seven days to write a single page."*
>
> — Winston Churchill

Now for a common sense lesson about how the customer is always right, even when wrong, from Jack Ferguson, CEO of the Philadelphia Convention and Visitors Bureau.

Years ago, at the Westin Cincinnati Hotel, when I was relatively new sales manager, I invited a corporate meeting planner to lunch. We had put the sales manager through excellent training and felt she could handle the luncheon appointment with the customer quite easily.

The customer (an extremely large man carrying a lot of weight) and the sales manager arrived at the hotel restaurant. Common sense would have steered both the hostess and the sales manager to seat the customer at the appropriate table or banquette. However, they pulled out an armchair and the customer took his seat.

Upon finishing lunch, when the customer went to get up, to everyone's horror, the chair stayed with him. As he went to push the chair free, both arms broke off and he stood there embarrassed, to say the least.

Common sense should have made both the hostess and sales manager escort the customer to the banquette. If the customer used good common sense, he should have said, "I prefer the banquette," but he did not, and like it or not, the customer is always right! Common sense used by the staff could have avoided the customer being embarrassed.

We did not book his meeting, and even after I left the hotel, we had not secured his account.

CS = PR² Lesson: The customer is right even when wrong.

Here is a great follow-up common sense example on how to build relationships from Jim Evans, former Vice President of Sales at Hyatt Hotels and Resorts.

When I think of my experience prior to joining Hyatt, I had received virtually no training from Sheraton and, I believe, I had been given the opportunities I had because of my outgoing personality and high energy—not because of any real selling experience. The direction I received was "Make sales calls"—lots of them! My general manager expected me to make 100 sales calls each week, and I did, making sure I called on every corporation, large and small, within a three- to five-mile radius of our Sheraton Northbrook Hotel.

In May 1975, I drove my car and all my possessions to Boston to start my new career with Hyatt Hotels and Resorts. Vice President of Sales Joe Kordsmeier was great to his team. If you worked hard and kept him updated on progress and problems, he let you do your thing. So, by summer's end, I had hired my team of four sales managers and (based on my Sheraton experience), I had each team member make lots of sales call in

Cambridge and its surrounding suburbs, including Boston—nothing very sophisticated.

In the fall of 1976, The American Society of Association Executives' annual convention (ASAE) came to Boston. Much to my surprise, Joe invited me to join his team at the conference. His direction was "Stay close to me or one of the other senior guys," so I was always standing next to Joe or a guy named John Russell, Director of Sales for the Hyatt Regency New Orleans. The show went by fast, and before he left town, Joe came by my office to greet my team and give them a bit of his enthusiastic support. After our sales meeting, he asked me how I had enjoyed ASAE. I think my answer disappointed him because for me the conference was a challenge. Even though Joe and John introduced me to many association executives (including Jim Low, President of ASAE), I was, nevertheless, the fifth wheel and always on the outside of every conversation.

Here is where common sense came to play. Joe sat with me for another thirty minutes and helped me put together a plan for next year's ASAE convention. He asked me how many business cards I had collected. I think it was twenty to twenty-five. His instruction was to write to every single one of those people, thanking them for their time, and to include a brochure for the Hyatt Regency Cambridge. I should then let them know that if they were coming to Boston in the next year to please let me know and I'd have a complimentary room waiting for them. Next, he told me to wait a month and then call each person's office and ask to speak with his or her assistant. My goal with each assistant was to learn something personal about each prospective client: birthday, favorite foods, sports they loved, etc.

"The reason a lot of people don't recognize an opportunity is because it usually goes around wearing coveralls looking like hard work."

— Thomas Edison

CS = PR² Lesson: Selling is the art of creating personal relationships and closing the deal.

Here are two wonderful common sense lessons from Brian Stevens, President of Conference Direct and former Vice President of Sales for Hilton Hotels and Resorts. It's about how to be creative with the sales process.

Lesson 1: Charles Slack (a customer) told me he liked champagne on the inbound drive from the airport. He had a tentative booking with us and the St. Francis Hotel (Westin). That night, I ordered a bottle of mid-priced French champagne. We had a toast and he said, "It's good, but not Dom." I went into the kitchen and ordered two bottles of Dom…. The next day, he rebooked the convention. My boss (Werner Lewin, General Manager of Hilton San Francisco) gave me a hard time about the restaurant check the next day. Then I handed him the signed contract and the boss shut up. True story. I got that sale in 1981. It taught me to be flexible.

Lesson 2: We had one presidential suite in the hotel…. It was taken by another group, but on the site inspection, the prospective customer said he wanted the presidential suite. Rather than to tell him it was not available, we took another suite that had the same square footage and renamed it the King Presidential Suite and called the original the Queen Presidential Suite…. Problem solved.

CS = PR²: Think outside the box. Be flexible and creative.

Now for some common sense lessons on where sales professionals go wrong in all types of enterprises.

Most Business Owners, Hotel Managers, Presidents, and CEOs are frustrated with:

1. Sales teams that are run like fraternities.

2. Sales managers who focus on poorly qualified pipelines instead of on closing deals and the bottom line.

3. Sales managers who rely on salesperson optimism instead of holding salespeople accountable to objective performance standards.

4. Salespeople blaming their poor sales results on a bad economy, bad leads, or other external factors.

5. Salespeople not being proactive in the selling process—not making cold calls, not confronting objections, not calling on/ meeting with top level decision-makers, not qualifying prospects before providing costly proposals.

6. Salespeople who are such social butterflies that they fail to see the signals and close the sale.

The sales process in the hotel business is best described by an inverted triangle.

- Customer/friend on the top axis
- Director or VP of Sales on left axis
- Conference service on the right axis
- President/CEO/hotel manager on the inverted point of the axis

An inverted triangle sample is in this chapter's appendix.

One may be gratified in the short term by a bad booking to make the sale—for example, booking rooms over the approved hotel room blocks, or quoting the wrong rates. Rest assured, the bad will live long after the bad sale is made, and with repercussions that could have a negative impact on a career.

You only make a bad sale once. In *Julius Caesar*, Shakespeare has Mark Antony say after Caesar is killed, "the good is oft interred in the bones but the bad lives after them."

CS = PR² Lesson: You only make a bad sale once!

Bruce Lucker, former Century Plaza Sales Team member and former CEO of Madison Square Gardens, offers our next common sense lesson, which illustrates: *Few if any battles are won by having customers eat crow. It will not turn into filet mignon.*

So there I was at the Americana of New York as the (young and very green) convention coordinator—1,853-room hotel with tons of meeting space.

One Monday, just before lunch, I received a frantic call in my office from a meeting planner who was on the Versailles Terrace watching the housemen crew set up her opening general session.

"Come up here immediately...please!" she yelled.

Skipping the elevator and scaling three steps down the stairway at a time, I entered the Versailles Terrace within a few moments of her call.

"How can I help you?" I asked her when I arrived.

She pointed to one of the three-foot wide pillars throughout the room (there were probably twelve) and screams, "You have to move those immediately! I have my opening luncheon starting within the hour and my guest speaker needs to be able to show his slides on a large screen. My guests will never be able to see the screen with these pillars in the room, so please move them now."

Well, I had to be the bearer of bad news that the pillars could not be moved since they helped to hold up the fifty-story building.

"What are you talking about?" she replied. "O'Reilly, the banquet manager, assured me the pillars were mobile when he booked my luncheon!"

What could I do but invite the meeting planner to join me at the closest pillar? I then placed both her hands on the pillar and suggested she push.

Well, she got the message and I got a lesson in how some people, regardless of their titles, sometimes just lack common sense.

*CS = PR² Lesson: You can make silk out of a cow's ear or
put a round peg in a square hole!*

Here's a final common sense pearl of wisdom from branding guru Duane Knapp:

Selling a service (a dream), creating the vision of a successful meeting, wedding, social event, is not an easy task that requires special skills. The salesperson must paint a picture in the mind's eye of the buyer that closes the deal.

It easy to offer the lowest rate (give it away) to make a sale. It is important that the Director of Sales set revenue and average rate goals in order to make the most profitable sale with the highest average rate (ADR) possible to maximize revenues and "flow through."

"If you can't give away try selling it."

— David R. Evans

An example of the key elements of a sales team can be found in this chapter's appendix.

CHAPTER SIX SALES TAKEAWAYS

Sales is an organizational function that builds relationships, *direct and indirect*, to introduce a product or service's value proposition. A successful sale is when a customer believes the proposed value proposition and purchases the product or service.

- Don't fish in an empty pond.
- Selling is the art of creating personal relationships and closing the deal. To close the deal, find the hot button. Think outside the box.
- Know the customer. Get all the facts beforehand. Ask, "What does it take to get your business?"
- Turning a client into a lifelong friend is the formula for successful selling.
- Dare to be different when establishing unique selling points (USP).
- It is better to act on our instincts than ask for forgiveness later. A unique USP can close the deal.
- Seek out the most dominant decision maker.
- You only make a bad sale once, and if you do this will come back to haunt you.
- Don't blame your sales team for poor results; look in the mirror. Don't punish for failure. Encourage and reward success. A pat on the back with a warm smile will win the day in the long run.

What are the three most important things you learned in this chapter?

1. _____

2. _____

3. _____

6

APPENDIX

THE DREA REVERSE MARKETING PLAN: KNOW THY ENEMY

The Reverse Marketing Plan (RMP) is a simple exercise that puts the sales team into the minds of the competitors. It requires the hotel sales marketing team to visit and prepare a sales and marketing plan for that hotel or product on how to sell and market it against its competitors.

It is one thing to identify and list the competitors; it is equally as important to understand how the competition views your product and would sell and market against you.

Elements of the RMP: A sample review matrix is listed below; the review categories are not set in concrete.

For example, a SWOT (Strengths, Weaknesses, Opportunities, and Threats) analysis is only part of the process. The team must develop and be aware of the tactics and strategies that the competitive hotels will use to gain market share advantage. Suggested categories to consider include:

- Operator
- Meeting space

- Restaurants
- Distribution
- Special Services
- Sales team profiles
- Advertising
- Public Relations
- Key customers (for targets)

A sample review matrix can be tailored for each review category. Scale: 1 to 5 (5 being the best)

Hotel	Curb Appeal	Lobby Décor	Front Desk Location	Front Desk Associate/ Decor	Restaurant Location	Function Space
Fairmont	4	4	5	5	4	5

Operator/ Brand	Position in the Market	RSO System	Distribution	Frequent Guest Program
Fairmont	5	3.5	3.5	2

Note: Sample only. This does not reflect a David R. Evans & Associates' analysis of this brand.

David R. Evans recommends that each member of the sales and catering team take one hotel a month for one year. For example, if there are six hotels in the competitive set, then each associate can take one every two months, and at the month-end sales meeting, give a presentation to the whole operations committee.

CHAPTER SIX SALES APPENDIX (2)

The Key Elements of a Successful Sales Team (DREA)

Element	Comments	Grade 1 to 5, 5 highest.
Communications: Sales associates are curious and like to be kept in the loop. Conduct regular sales meetings. These dates must be sacred.		
Financial Information: The better the knowledge of the P&L and "Flow Through," the better the opportunity for improved revenue.		
Empowerment: Your competitor loves it when you tie down your associates with reports.		
Office Environment: Good working conditions convert to increased performance and production.		
Know Your Competition: Know them just as well as you know your property, and don't disturb the competition while they are making mistakes.		
Sales Training: Keep your team on the cutting edge.		
Adequate Staff and Support Systems: Incentives are a must in today's marketplace. Create reasonable and measurable goals. "What gets measured gets done."		

Element	Comments	Grade 1 to 5, 5 highest.
Know the Competition: How are they selling against you? Conduct regular "Reverse Marketing Plans."		
Kick the Tires: Think outside the box, set aside productive planning "think" time		
Encourage Continuous Improvement: Training, Industry Involvement.		
Create a Good Environment: A good environment encourages balance between work, family, and play. Associates are no good to the organization if they are in the hospital.		
Recognition and Support by Senior Management: Sales associates thrive on a pat on the back and "Atta boy/girl" commendations.		

"Selling is the art of closing the business and making the deal. The sale begins with no!"

— David R. Evans

COMMON SENSE CS = PR²

FINAL NOTE

I was truly blessed to have had my incredible thirty-nine wonderful years at Western International Hotels and its successive companies. I was in the right place at the right time in the evolution of hotel sales and marketing from 1961 to 2000. The lessons learned from my bosses, associates, competitors, and customers were the catalyst for my career advancement from novice to senior vice president.

I put the lessons learned during my active career to good use after I retired.

In 2002, with the wise counsel of my long-time friend and former associate David Brudney (David Brudney and Associates), I formed David R. Evans & Associates (DREA). David and I worked with several convention bureaus, and I advised owners (e.g., Vulcan—Pan Pacific Seattle) and developers. I also created my CS = PR² DREA Road Map to Success.

I wish for you just as rich and rewarding a career and life. But before you go, I have a few last things to share with you that hopefully can aid you in creating a future filled with common sense.

DAVID R. EVANS' DEFINITION OF LUCK

L...

Luck: When planning meets opportunity mixed with being in the right place at the right time.

Love: The family, they come first.

Love of Life: Don't shortchange yourself. Take full advantage of life's experiences and don't sweat the small stuff.

Leisure: Put balance in your life.

U...

Understanding: Do unto others because we are all unique. Treat your associates, friends, and competitors honestly, fairly, and with humility. What goes around comes around.

C...

Courage: Take a chance; put your stake in the sand. Don't sit on the sidelines. Strive to make a difference. Let your intuition be your guide. The worst three words in the English language are "I should have."

Caring: Consider the less fortunate and give back.

Commitment: To your family, your customer, your employer, and your country.

K...

Knowledge: Life is a voyage—a constant learning experience. Share your knowledge and become a mentor. History is the road map to the future.

THE SHORT RULES OF LIFE

- Life is short.
- Break the rules.
- Forgive quickly.
- Love truly.
- Laugh uncontrollably.
- Never regret anything that made you smile.
- Loyal friends are hard to come by so don't lose them.
- If you know the enemy and know thyself, you need not fear one hundred battles. (Sun Tzu)
- The best things in life are free, until the government finds out and taxes them.
- Answer all emails and return all phone calls. The email or call you don't return may fire you one day. The call or email you return may hire you one day.

Thank you for investing your time in reading *The Power of Common Sense*. Now that you have finished this book, how will you challenge yourself to apply its advice?

Take a few minutes now to list the top ten things you have learned from reading this book:

1. _____

2. _____

3. _____

4. _____

5. _____

6. _____

7. _____

8. _____

9. _____

10. _____

Now create a list of the top ten actions you will take to enhance your life or career as a result of reading this book. If appropriate, apply the advice from your list above to create your action steps.

1. _____

2. _____

3. _____

4. _____

5. _____

6. _____

7. _____

8. _____

9. _____

10. _____

I hope reading *The Power of Common Sense* has given you the wisdom and encouragement to take action now to improve your life. However, if you need any assistance, feel free to contact me. I would love to lock arms with you and serve as your mentor and advisor to help you and your organization achieve your goals. Therefore, I would like to offer you a complimentary thirty-minute consultation by phone to discuss how I might assist you. You can contact me at:

206-930-7087
huskees@comcast.net
www.davidrevanschme.com

Dave R. Evans
May you be blessed in all your endeavors!

Yesterday is history.
Today is a gift.
Tomorrow is a mystery.
HAVE A GREAT DAY!

ACKNOWLEDGMENTS

I wish to thank all those who took the time to respond to my request for assistance with this book:

This is a sample of my common sense request to former associates, competitors, and customers prior to starting my book.

I would like to ask a favor and assistance on a personal project I am about to undertake.

We grew up in the hospitality industry more often than not by the seat of our pants, learning from others, using our common sense and chutzpah to build relationships, close the deal, and work with our team members, associates, bosses, competitors, and suppliers.

I have noticed in the past ten years that using good common sense seems to have been replaced with a total lack of common sense. Common sense has gone the way of political correctness, and in the process, the only winners today seems to be lawyers.

I was moved to this belief by a good friend who suggested I read *Common Sense* by Thomas Paine, written in 1775 and used by Thomas Jefferson to create The Declaration of independence. In forty-five pages, Paine successfully created the rationale for the greatest democratic experiment ever.

I started to put together an anthology of common sense lessons I have learned from good friends like you, and from customers, family, and life experiences over the forty-year span of my active career.

So I would like to impose on your good mind and assistance by requesting from you a common sense example or examples.

Tell me where in your career, business, or personal life, you experienced a lack of common sense that later backfired, or when a simple or complex task or issue could have been solved with some good common sense.

I don't want to burden you with writing a long paper. A paragraph or two will suffice.

I am not sure how the finished product will look, but every walk begins with a first step. I intend to list the examples by author so you receive credit for them.

If you can get something back to me by mid-June 2013, that would be helpful. If you have any questions, please let me know, or if you won't have something to send me, please let me know that as well.

Thank you and best wishes,

Dave R. Evans

LIST OF CONTRIBUTORS:

Chapter One
Tony Schopp
Brian Hornyak

Chapter Two
David Brudney
Harry Mullikin
Dan McClaskey
August Busch
Cindy Novotny
Brian Stevens
Duane Knapp

Chapter Three
Alfred Evans (My Father)
Katherine Evans (My Mother)
Roy Evans
David Noonan
Akio Hirao
David Brudney
Peter Rozelle
August Busch
Jim McFarland
Kenzo Tenge

Chapter Four
Fred Kleisner
Steve Halliday
Eddie Carlson
Larry Dustin
Don Freeman
Jack Vaughn
Larry Magnan

Chapter Five
Roy Evans
Clyde Harris
Sig Front
Doug Ducate

Chapter Six
Andy Finn
Peter Smith
George Caldwell
Duane Knapp

I would also like to thank the wonderful management and support team at the Century Plaza, who made me and our sales team look very good by turning our clients into lifelong friends. Thanks go to:

- Harry Mullikin, Managing Director
- Dan McClaskey, Resident Manager
- T. Peter Blyth, Food and Beverage Director, providing twenty-four room service

- William D. Ellis, Controller, who paid our expense accounts without a whimper
- George Williams and Larry Magnan, Front Office Managers
- Bodo Lemke, "World Class Convention Service Manager"
- Gina Tucker, Executive Housekeeper. Gina is "one of a kind." She created folded toilet paper and nightly turn-down service
- Walter Roth, Executive Chef, "Creator of the American Culinary program"
- Frank Aprent, Banquet Headwaiter, "The best banquet service in the country"
- All the Beefeater doormen who were our first line of exceptional service

The Stellar Century Plaza Hotel Sales Team
- David Brudney
- David Falor
- Jack O'Hara
- Pat O'Daniel
- Stan Soroka
- Linda Sperber

The exceptional sales support team.

Charlene Chabin, my administrative assistant, who helped kept me out of trouble.

Thank you all for these wonderful years in the world of hospitality, where I received a PhD in Life Smarts on the streets of Los Angeles, and learned lessons from many friends, customer, colleagues, and celebrities whom I was privileged to meet upfront and personal.

Thank-you Rachel Langaker, and the Fusion Creative Works team for an outstanding job with cover and interior book design.

Thank you also to Westin Hotels and Resorts Global Regional Sales Team:

London
   Michael Andrea
   Michael Holehouse
   Valerie Le Moignan

Frankfurt
   Andre Shober

Washington, DC
   Roger Smith
   Tony Schop
   Bob Bushman

San Francisco
   Paula Crowder

Toronto
   Brian Hornyak

Tokyo
   Akio Hirao
   Hiro Kobyashi

Paris
   Ann Fracouis Bloten

New York City
   Clyde Harris
   Rick Hansen

Los Angeles
   Sherm Elliott

Special thanks to Jim Weiss, Director of Corporate Market Segment. Special thanks also to Marsha Massey, Manager of the Tour and Travel Market Segment

My appreciation goes to the extraordinary officers at Western International Hotels who kept me on my toes with common sense lessons every day.

- Lynn Himmelman, Chairman
- Gordon Bass, President
- Bob Lindquist, President
- Joe Calihan, Senior VP
- Joe Mogush, Senior VP
- Ralph Van Noy, VP
- Bill Kiethan, Senior VP Development
- Ken Mallory, VP

Associations

Thank you to the many wonderful association executives we served at the Century Plaza and who became dear friends over the years:

- Jim Lowe and R. William Taylor, Executive VPs, American Society of Association Executives
- Roy B. Evans, CEO Professional Convention Management Association
- Deborah Sexton, CEO Professional Convention Management Association
- Ed Griffin, CEO Meeting Planners International
- Frank Berkman, Executive VP Hotel Sales Manager Associations
- John Grey, National Asphalt Pavement Association
- John Barrett, American Trucking Association
- Bob Hobart, American Medical Association
- Bob Donovan, American Hospital Association
- Bob Hobart, American Hospital Association
- Tony Jannetti, Owner, Jannetti and Associates
- Bill Nelligan, American College of Cardiology
- David Noonan, American College Ophthalmology

...Corporations/Sports:

- August Busch III and Keith Fowler, Anheuser-Busch
- Lynn Townsend, CEO, Chrysler
- Henry Ford III, CEO, Ford Motor Company
- Bob Tiffany, Executive VP, Equitable Life
- Robert Clausen, CEO, Bank of America
- Robert Wood, CEO, CBS Affiliate Meetings Director
- Leonard Goldenson, CEO, NBC
- Mike Laurence, Affiliate Director, NBC
- Elton Rule, CEO, ABC
- Milton Carney, Affiliate Meetings Director, ABC
- Tommy Lasorda, LA Dodgers

- Daryl Royal, UW Husky Football Coach
- Jim Owens, UW Husky Football Coach
- Don James, UW Husky Football Coach
- Elmer Nordstrom, Seahawk Original Owner
- Mike Holmgren, Seahawks Head Coach
- Chuck Knox, Seahawks Head Coach
- Tex Schram, Dallas Cowboys Exec VP
- Gil Brandt, Dallas Cowboys, Director of Player Personnel
- Pete Rozelle, Commissioner NFL, and Carrie Rozelle, spouse
- Don Weiss, NFL Executive VP
- Jim Steeg, NFL Director, Super Bowl
- Bill Sullivan, Owner, New England Patriots
- Tommy Lasorda, Manager, LA Dodgers
- Merlin Olsen, NFL Hall of Famer
- John Meyers, Owner, Seattle Coors Beer Distributor, and Best Friend

...Politics
- George Bush, US President
- Ronald Reagan, California Governor
- Sam Yorty, LA Mayor

...Prince Hotels
- Sumio Furagawa, General Manager
- Ken Kishi, Prince Meetings Coordinator
- Eiju Oshima, Resident Manager
- Kenso Tange, Architect

...Advertising and Marketing
- Duane Knapp, Brand Strategy
- Jim McFarland, Partner McFarland Richards
- Jerry Rashal, Specialty Advertising
- Ross and Ann Heller, Publisher USAE

...Pan Pacific Seattle Hotel

- Paul Allen, Owner, Vulcan
- Ada Healy, VP Real Estate
- Gary Zak, Hotel Asset Manager
- Steve Halliday, SVP Pan Pacific Hotels and Resorts
- Lori Magro, Hotel GM (Opening)
- Lloyd Daser, Hotel Interim GM
- David Sullivan, Hotel GM
- Kevin Croley, SVP Marketing Pan Pacific Hotels and Resorts

...And Hollywood

- Lorne Greene, Actor, CPH Frequent guest
- Gregory Peck, Actor, President of the Screen Actors Guild, which met frequently at the CPH
- Daryl F. Zanuck, CEO, 20th Century Fox, CPH Frequent Guest
- Monte Hall, President, Friar's Club, Beverly Hills
- Gene Autry, Owner, Autry Hotels
- Kirk Douglas, Actor, CPH Frequent Guest
- John Wayne, Actor and Friend
- Cliff Robertson, Actor, Santa Monica Honorary Mayor

... And Competitors/Hotel Sales and Marketing Professionals

- Roger Dow, SVP Marketing, Marriott
- Jim Evans, VP Sales, Hyatt
- Don Pritzker, Owner, Hyatt
- Skip Friend, Executive VP, Hyatt
- Daryl Hartley, CEO, Leonard Hyatt
- Conrad Hilton, CEO, Hilton
- Walter Potts, Regional Director of Sales, Hilton
- Jim Collins, VP, Hilton Sales
- Charlotte St. Martin, VP of Sales, Lowes Hotels
- George Harbaugh, VP of Sales, Biltmore LA and Riviera Palm Springs

- Ed Sansovini, Principal, Ed Sansovini and Associates; President, Hotel Sales Management Association (HSMA)
- Sig Front, Senior VP Sales and Marketing Sahara Hotel Los Vegas
- Charlie Monahan, Senior VP Sales and Marketing, Caesar's Palace
- John Monahan, Senior VP Sales and Marketing, Diplomat Hotel Miami
- Lou Rogers, Senior VP, Fontainebleau Miami
- Benny Gould, VP Sales, Biltmore LA
- Frank Widman, VP Sales, Ambassador Hotel LA
- Don Welch, CEO, Destination Management International
- Tom Norwalk, CEO, Visit Seattle
- John Metcalf, Sales, Fairmont SFO and Founder of Associated Luxury Hotels
- Fred Kleisner, President Westin (Starwood Hotels and Resorts)

I am having a senior moment as I wrap up my seven-year book project, so I apologize to anyone who may be missing from this list. I give them a tip of my hat and my thanks for helping me learn my common sense lessons throughout my career.

Finally, I will be forever grateful for my wonderful book coach Patrick Snow, a stellar advisor and author of *Creating Your Own Destiny*. He was my guiding light and mentor on this project. Thank you also to leadership trainer Theresa Callahan, who was my inspiration for this book.

"What shall it profit a man,
if he gains the whole world
and loses his own soul?"

— MARK 8:36

ABOUT THE AUTHOR

DAVID R. EVANS, CHME

Born, Vancouver, BC, Canada

Raised in Caulfield, West Vancouver, BC.

1954-1955: Worked summers at The Harrison Hot Springs Resort located 60 miles east of Vancouver, BC. Started cleaning the kitchen, had a short stint at the front desk, then was promoted to bellman.

1955: Graduated from West Vancouver High School. Played rugby and basketball.

1955: Came to the US via a football scholarship at Wenatchee Valley College in central Washington.

1956: Recruited to University of Washington by Daryl Royal, who after one year became head coach at the University of Texas. I decided to stay one more year at Wenatchee Valley College.

1957-1959: Odd jobs including loading box cars with apples in Chelan, Washington.

1959: Entered the University of Washington. Majored in radio and TV production, with a minor in advertising and public relations.

1961: Graduated with a BA in Communications.

1961: Good fortune prevailed. Mrs. Bullett, the owner of KING-TV, Seattle's first TV station, decided to add two interns, who were radio and TV majors at the University of Washington's School of Communications to her production team. I was fortunate to be one of the two selected. It was a job made in heaven for a wannabe film director. That summer was an incredible job experience.

1961: While at KING-TV, I learned of an opening in public relations at Seattle's premier hotel, The Olympic Hotel. I decided to interview, thinking that during a short stint at this wonderful hotel, I would meet someone who would pull me through the glass ceiling to obtain one of the hard-to-get production jobs in Hollywood.

1961: My hotel experience at Harrison Hot Springs was instrumental in getting hired at Western International Hotels for a hotel sales job. I would retire thirty-nine years later.

1964: I was selected to be part of the pre-opening sales team, for the new Century Plaza Hotel by Harry Mullikin, Managing Director. This spectacular hotel would be in the former backlot of Twentieth Century Fox Studios, the Aluminum Company of America (ALCOA) development in West Los Angeles.

1966: (June) Promoted to Director of Sales for the Century Plaza Hotel.

1969-1971: President of the Hotel Sales Managers Association of Southern California.

1969-71: Served on the board of the International Board of Directors Hotel Sales Managers Association.

1971: Named "National Hotel Salesman of the Year" in a national competition sponsored by the Hotel School at Washington State University, Pullman, Washington.

1973: Promoted to Vice President-General Sales Manager. Moved to Western International Hotels' (WIH) Seattle Headquarters.

1975: Assume responsibilities for oversight of Western International Hotels' Global Sales Offices.

1977: Selected to be the hotel industry's member of the American Society of Association Executives (ASAE) Board of Directors. Only one person from the hotel industry is selected for this honor.

1978: Selected to represent the hotel industry on the Board of Directors for the Professional Convention Managers Association (PCMA).

1980: Selected to serve on the Executive Committee of the Professional Convention Management Association (PCMA) by PCMA Board President Brad Claxton, Executive Vice President of the American Academy of Dermatologists. I was the first hotelier to be selected for this prestigious position.

1983: Western International Hotels has a branding change to Westin. Westin will become the dominant hotel brand in the upper upscale hotel segment with the value proposition "People make the difference."

1994: Aoki Corporation, Tokyo, Japan, buys Westin.

1997: Barry Sternlicht, real estate developer, buys Westin. He creates a new industry brand, Starwood Hotels and Resorts.

1998: Sternlicht adds Sheraton to the Starwood Portfolio.

1998: I'm named, Senior Vice President of Industry Relations for Starwood Hotels and Resorts, reporting to President Fred Kleisner.

2000: (March) I take early retirement due to a heart transplant.

2000 (March 31): The Seattle Westin Offices close forever. All functions move to Starwood Hotels and Resorts, Headquarters in White Plains, New York.

Recognitions for Service to the Hotel Industry

- Hotel Sales Manager of the Year: Washington State Hotel School National Competition
- American Society of Executives (ASAE): Academy of Leaders

- Convention Liaison Council (CLC): Hall of Leaders
- Hotel Sales Manager International Association (HSMA): Certified Hotel Marketing Executive (CHME) and Hall of Fame
- Meeting Professionals International (MPI): President's Award
- Professional Convention Management Association (PCMA): Distinguished Service Award, Professional Achievement Award, and Lifetime Achievement Award

Today, David R. Evans is semi-retired but still operating his consulting business.

Visit David at **www.DavidREvansCHME.com**